The Change Maker

The Change Maker

Preserving the Promise of America

Al Checchi

OPEN ROAD

INTEGRATED MEDIA

NEW YORK

To
Kathy, of course, and Adam, Kristin, and Kate,
and all who paved the road to opportunity for us.

When you come to a fork in the road, take it.

Yogi Berra

Contents

Preface

I CAME OF AGE in a muscular and dynamic America that was the envy of the world. It was a country of unmatched vision, promise, and inspiration during the early 1960s, but violent social and political upheaval as the decade closed. It was a time when great leaders dared incite us to higher levels of innovation, achievement, and service for the greater good of country. But when several of those leaders fell to assassins' bullets and we became mired in a controversial war, a generation of Americans lost faith in government and our elected officials. Since that time we have been participants in technological revolution and social devolution, economic boom and dot-com bust, and political swings left, right, and back again, and our disaffection with government has grown. Yet despite all this upheaval and the rapid pace of change, I found one constant: Leadership matters.

My career in business, and indeed much of my life, has been the study and practice of leadership. Each enterprise with which I engaged and every person with whom I worked taught me lessons in the value of forceful and responsible leadership. I have seen the power of great leaders to transform institutions and the power of poor, self-interested leaders to destroy them. I have seen government lift us up when its leaders have vision, courage, and imagination, and I have witnessed uninspired, irresponsible leadership hobble our country economically and diminish its standing in the world. Yet as I have traveled through this country, I have been elevated by the level of volunteerism, faith, and determination of our people. Invariably, they yearn and hope for a return to a better time when we shared the burdens of democracy and affirmed the promise of the American Dream.

Our country suffers from a leadership crisis. Too many private-sector leaders have abdicated their fiduciary responsibilities and become parasites on their clients, customers, and shareholders. In the public sector, our politics have been hijacked by a cadre of self-perpetuating careerists devoid of the substantive experience and acquired skill necessary to lead our country during this time of unique challenge. As our society has become more complex, we have become more interdependent, and institutional power has become more concentrated. Accordingly, the wisdom and skill of our leaders—and their commitment and fidelity as stewards—are more important than ever.

I have written this book because I am concerned that the fundamental promise of America is in peril. The uninterrupted record of each successive generation creating a higher standard of living for the next, our continued ability to assure individual opportunity, and our position of global preeminence hang in the balance. Understanding the role of strong leadership and its power to transform our public and private institutions is the key to rebuilding our country and maintaining our position as the world's indispensable nation.

PART I

ONE
Salinas, 1998

S ALINAS ON A HOT and dusty afternoon seemed as good a place as any
to end my campaign for the Democratic nomination for governor of
California. Six days out from the June 2, 1998 primary, after nearly two
and a half years of research and planning, hundreds of speeches, thousands of miles, countless meetings, and the investment of nearly $40 mil-
lion of my own personal funds, the bright yellow school bus that had
become the rolling symbol of my candidacy pulled off the highway and
immediately took a wrong turn.

No one had said that success would be easy, and after three generations in the New World, the Checchi family knew something about struggling. The path to upward mobility had been paved with hard work and
heartache. Because of the sacrifices made by my immigrant grandparents
and parents, I had full access to the American Dream. I had been taught
to work hard and play by the rules. And I had been extremely lucky. I
was given the opportunity to participate in the transformation of three
of America's largest institutions; achieved national recognition as a corporate innovator and leader; and soared into the upper reaches of the
Forbes 400. And in California in 1998, I brazenly challenged the political
establishment of America's most populous state. But here I was, one week
shy of my fiftieth birthday, crammed into the seat of a school bus. Lost.
And going . . . nowhere.

Less than two hours earlier, Darry Sragow, my campaign manager, had phoned in the numbers that confirmed my breathtaking drop from first place among the Democratic challengers.

I had achieved a statistically significant lead in the Democratic field just four weeks prior, but there had been clear warnings since then that my primary opponents' major blitz of paid advertising was taking its toll. "This has become a race for second place," said Darry. "That's what we're facing."

My wife, Kathy, and I spent a few minutes alone in the windowless office where we'd received the news to compose ourselves. We talked about how to tell the many volunteers, who had worked so hard for so long to help us, that we could not succeed. There was nothing for us to do now but what we had been doing for almost two and a half years, and indeed for most of our twenty-five years of marriage: "Keep on keeping on," as the Bob Dylan song says. We had achieved success, and we had tasted failure. We had turned defeat into victory and victory into defeat. This would be a defeat, a large one. But as always, there would be no excuses, no whining, and no quitting.

My wife, Kathy, and me on the campaign trail.

Why did I run?

California has always been the place where Americans came to fulfill their dreams, whether in the image-factories of Hollywood or the high-tech companies of the Silicon Valley. As the laboratory of the American Dream, California is where America continually reinvents, rejuvenates, and renews itself. The state's leaders and citizens had shared a vision and commitment to bearing the collective cost of creating opportunity and investing in the future.

However, over the previous two decades, California had lost this animating spirit and, with it, its preeminence. California was no longer prepared to cultivate its population with the schools and infrastructure investment needed to make it a more prosperous place for all.

The state that had developed the best public education system in the nation and led the country in the construction of highways and ports, whose extensive waterworks system had even transformed its vast deserts into fields of plenty, was now dead last among all fifty states, in terms of public infrastructure investment. To anyone who had traveled the world, as I most certainly had as the former chairman of an international airline, the decline in California's infrastructure, particularly its public education system, reflected the failure of our entire country to keep pace with the public and private investments that were surging in countries like China, Japan, India, and Korea. California—and America—was losing the race for the future.

This "Mississippification" of California, as one pithy scholar dubbed it, was accompanied by soaring juvenile- and violent-crime rates and falling per-capita income. Additionally, California, which had always struggled with immigration—whether the Chinese who built the railroads, Dust Bowl refugees of the 1930s, or African Americans from the Cotton Belt—was once again uneasy with the latest wave of immigrants from Mexico and points south. These issues, too, were becoming increasingly contentious all across America.

For hundreds of years, America and its most populous state have attracted the very best of human capital—the world's risk-takers, adventurers, and strivers—people willing to forsake the relative comfort of home and country and take a chance to seek and build a better life.

We have evolved a distinct, even an exceptional American culture. Time and again, as a country we have demonstrated our capacity for producing unmatched growth, unrivaled prosperity, and innovation limited only by imagination. We are protected by and enjoy the enormous benefits of the world's most enlightened and enduring constitution, buttressed by an extensive network of public and private institutions that support, nurture, and facilitate the actualization of human potential, while safeguarding our most unalienable rights.

I had entered the race for governor of California because I found it incomprehensible that a state and, by extension, a country so magnificently endowed could be allowed to fail so unnecessarily. Given such an extraordinary base of human and material resources, I felt that I could lead the process of change necessary to restore California's positive trajectory and so set an example for the entire country.

I built a career based on the belief that leadership matters. A belief that the ability to enlist and inspire others in a shared vision, manage and direct human and material resources to achieve agreed-upon ends, and actualize human potential is the most powerful force in affecting the human condition. Throughout my career, in various capacities, I had seen leaders effect change—to observe, analyze, consult, create, plan, recruit, and execute to produce significant and measurable results. This was how I had seen change happen—not with slogans, but with action. This was how I drew upon experiences, built skills, and developed my own modest history of achieved results. To my way of thinking, nothing material had changed in California. The resources were still there, the human capital continued to be plentiful, the cultural foundation and institutions remained in place.

What had happened, however, was a massive decline in the capacities, motivations, and ethics of our leaders: political, economic, and social. During my career, I have seen numerous institutions rise, fall, and rise again based solely on changes in leadership. I also had witnessed a general decline in the fiduciary character of our leadership, that most essential prerequisite to the beneficial exercise of individual power. It seemed clear to me that California and America were continuing to endow their leaders with enormous and increasing power, and that those leaders exercised that power with increasingly less regard for the interests of the citizenry.

That hot afternoon in Salinas, we were, as we had been in so many other places around the state, trying to focus attention and shine light, pose the right questions, expose the problems, propose solutions, and enlist others in a crusade to reclaim and renew America's preeminence. The Salinas Boys and Girls Club, adjacent to a public elementary school, was a model for the state. It offered after-school programs for low-income children, who were showing noteworthy improvements in academic performance.

As our yellow bus drove into view, the orderly formation of schoolchildren that had been arranged on the grass dissolved and surged toward the sidewalk. Here was a different and welcome rhythm: the frenzied energy of a well-attended campaign event.

An advance man waved the bus to a stop and grabbed a box of *The Checchi Plan*, the ninety-page tract outlining my detailed strategy for shepherding California into the twenty-first century.

As Kathy and I stepped off the bus, four television cameras bobbed above the heads of the children, who waved their hands and squealed, "Check-key, Check-key." At least here in Salinas we would be engulfed by the impetus for our campaign, the bright and shiny faces of young schoolchildren, the future of California and the nation.

The cameras were there only to record another in a series of campaign stops; but we hoped they would also shine some light on the needs and potential of these children.

The club director ushered us through the crowd of children ranging in age from eight to thirteen. They tugged at our clothes, offered high-fives, and asked for autographs. We were led into an area that had been set up for the children to do crafts. The television crews circled the conversation with lenses and microphones, but they did not remain passive for long. A correspondent in a bright red dress interrupted the scene, citing the deadline for the early newscasts. The whole press corps leaned in, en masse, for their important sound bite: my assessment of the political race and what I planned to do in the final week of the campaign. I dutifully but half-heartedly complied. I hadn't come to Salinas to talk about campaign mechanics.

The cameras had left by the time the Boys and Girls Club staffers calmed the children, corralling about sixty of them in an asphalt courtyard for a conversation about the school and the club programs. The children sat in a triangular patch of shade cast by the wall, each one clutching a copy of *The Checchi Plan*, several of them employing it as a makeshift fan.

I began:

"Do you see all these buildings here?" I pointed to the library and classrooms ringing the dusty playground.

"Do you see all the people who are here? All this is here—and all these people are here—because you are special.

"Here and at school, you get to learn some pretty great things. You get the chance to learn what you are good at. You also get the chance to learn what your friends are good at. You see how you are different and how you are alike. You also get to learn what people can do when they work together. You learn about history—what happened long ago and how we got to be where we are today. This is a good way to learn where you are going.

"I am running for governor of California, and if I win, I want to make sure that everyone has a club just like yours. This is the kind of place that I would like to see in other parts of California, and that's what this book is about," I said, pointing to *The Checchi Plan*. "I have written down ideas of what we should do to make every school as good as this one."

Having dazzled these children with my oratory, I then took questions:

"What's a governor?"

"Where do you live?"

"Do you have any children?"

"What do they do?"

All of which I answered to their apparent satisfaction.

Then a girl in a flowered dress, her dark hair pulled back into a ponytail, raised her hand.

"But have you ever worked in the fields?"

I looked at the faces arrayed in front of me. They were expectant. Not one seemed surprised by the question. The fields were an integral part of their lives.

I had been all over the state, spoken to thousands of people, in countless venues, and nobody had ever asked this question:

Have you ever worked in the fields?

Yet to understand these children and their lives, and those of their parents and uncles and aunts and older brothers, sisters and cousins, you had to understand leaving your native country, rising long before dawn, being away from family and loved ones, sometimes for weeks at a time, toiling in the sun and the heat, and earning wages barely sufficient to put food on the table and shelter and clothe your family. You had to understand migrant housing—dormitory-style, with scant privacy, poor sanitation, no sense of permanency—schools that changed with the seasons, addresses that rotated with the crops.

Had I ever worked in the fields?

My circumstances were such that I never experienced the hardship of that type of work, but I knew these people. My great-grandparents had worked in the fields: in Italy as farmers, and on the sea as fishermen, and in this country doing backbreaking manual labor. They, too, had braved the challenge of trying to establish themselves and assimilate into a new land. They had worked in the fields, so that their children and their children's children would not have to.

Win or lose—and by the time I rolled into Salinas, I was surely headed for defeat—the reason I had run for governor of California was to sound the alarm that we had to change our ways. We could not continue to vest power over our lives and the futures of our children in the hands of the political careerists who were running the state and country into the ground. I had run because I saw the need for change. I had run to prepare the way for a better future for California, and especially for the forgotten Californians: those who had come to harvest hope, those working in the fields.

Two
Beginnings

Send these, the homeless, tempest-tost, to me,
I lift my lamp beside the golden door!

Emma Lazarus

M Y FATHER'S PARENTS, ATTILIO Checchi and Dina Pisani, landed in
Boston during the great Italian and Irish migrations of the early
twentieth century. They had come, separately, from the same rocky out-
cropping in the Tyrrhenian Sea, Porto Azzuro, on the island of Elba.
Home to olive groves, goats, and generations of fishermen, Elba had
remained essentially unchanged for centuries. Its feudal economy offered
little more opportunity to people of modest ambition than it had the
rapacious Napoleon, its most famous exile.

My grandmother Dina, who was the matriarch of our family and
one of my greatest influences, stepped ashore in Boston with her mother
and two young brothers on the Commonwealth Pier in 1912, when she
was fourteen. They had departed Elba before receiving the final letter
of my great-grandfather, Alfredo, who had preceded his family a year
earlier. "Stay home," he wrote in that missive. "America is not what we
expected."

The streets of the New World, he had found, were not paved with gold, but rather littered with sorrow. His heartache for a missed home-land was compounded by slums, discrimination, prejudice, and a new and difficult language. Work was scarce; once found, it often paid little.

While Elba had been a place of narrow hopes and opportunities, it was also a familiar place of beauty, refinement, and repose, of fields tilled since time immemorial and churches with marble steps worn smooth by centuries of devotion.

America, on the other hand, was raw energy and motion. It offered opportunity, but only to those who overcame its brutal rites of initiation. And Boston, with its cold tenement flats and bare-knuckle politics, was a particularly forbidding place at the dawn of the twentieth century. No matter how circumscribed the life left behind, it was infinitely more certain than that produced by the competing cultures grasping for a foot-hold in the New World.

But my grandfather's warning had arrived too late. The family was reunited, and there would be no turning back. They would have to keep on keeping on. What drove them forward, however, was not just the circumstance of their arrival, but the evolving belief in the promise of America that drives all its initiates. The gap between that promise and the reality of life here had seemed so vast that at first my great-grandfather had perceived it as unbridgeable and sought to turn back. Yet, for new immigrants struggling to adapt, America offered the potent tonic of hope, the unshakeable and distinctly American belief in a better tomorrow. So, fortified by this potent elixir, the Pisanis of Boston, like millions before them, began the process of becoming Americans.

The family settled into a crowded apartment on Chelsea Street in East Boston, just a few blocks from the bustling waterfront and mariners' hotels of Maverick Square. Their life in East Boston was the hard life of factory workers. As my father used to say, "My family arrived in East Boston poor, and we left poor."

School was an unaffordable luxury. Young Dina found work dipping chocolates at the Cynthia Sweets confectioner's factory along the East Boston waterfront. It was monotonous, backbreaking work, but since she had more refined talents (her mother had taught knitting, lacemaking, and embroidery in Elba), she soon found employment at a fashionable dressmaker's shop on Newbury Street. She took the penny ferry ride each day across the harbor, but saved on trolley fare by daily walking the five-mile round trip from the North End docks to Copley Square.

The store owners and patrons appreciated my grandmother's fine embroidery work, but she soon learned that she earned half as much as less talented, more assimilated seamstresses who spoke English. In the first, but by no means last, act of family defiance in the New World, this young girl—my Nona, by far the most talented seamstress in the shop—confronted the owners, winning not only a raise, but back wages as well. She was on her way to pursuing the American Dream.

Several years later, Attilio Checchi paid a courtesy call on the Pisani family, whom he had known in Elba. He himself had immigrated to Boston earlier in 1905. He, too, had landed an apprenticeship dipping chocolates, and after a series of other odd jobs, he learned of an Italian family that needed help running their fruit and vegetable store in Saint Stephen in New Brunswick, Canada. Attilio moved there, and when the owners decided to return to Italy, he and his brother Tonino took over the store.

On his visit to Boston, the thirty-five-year-old Attilio casually asked my great-grandmother about her "cute little girl, Dina," whom he had not seen since she was five. It was not long after he laid eyes on the beautiful eighteen-year-old that Attilio and Dina were married. Attilio surrendered his interest in the Canadian store to his brother, and the newlyweds began their lives together in Calais, Maine, where they opened their own store, named in honor of their homeland, the Elba Fruit Market.

Calais wasn't then, and isn't now, the Maine of Bar Harbor and North Haven—loon-haunted summer enclaves for New York bankers and the First Families of Boston—but a hard-working lumber town of approximately six thousand. The move to a small, remote town where they were isolated from the immigrant-packed ghettos of the big city required rapid assimilation of my grandparents' family into their adopted land.

The Elba Fruit Market, circa 1922.

Attilio kept the inventory and Dina, who displayed a remarkable affinity for numbers, kept the books. I recall my grandmother poring over the store ledger, seeking to divine profit, loss, and opportunity in the rows of figures. I've often thought of her in the course of my own career, built in part by a similar flair for analysis.

Neither Attilio nor Dina ever attained more than a sixth-grade education. Nor did they ever really master English. But they knew that learning would pave the road to the opportunity they had never had. It was a lesson they reinforced continuously with their children. From the earliest age, my father and uncle were drilled in the value of education and encouraged in their schoolwork. The long hours at the store ingrained in them the work ethic that is the legacy of every successful immigrant family. Both brothers excelled in school and were admitted to the University of Maine.

Like the store, education was a family enterprise. My father and uncle both worked at the Elba Market while supporting each other through school, at times alternating semesters off from college to ensure the continued operation of both the Checchi family business and their respective educations.

My mother inherited the same conviction about learning. Her parents, Gemma and Arturo Soldati, from a farming village near Parma in the Romagna region in Northern Italy, were married there in 1907 and immigrated the same year to the United States, settling near cousins in Somersworth, New Hampshire. Having lost one child to disease during the Atlantic crossing and three more to a host of childhood maladies common in that pre-penicillin era, they shepherded the remaining seven Soldati children through high school at a time when most teenagers in the predominately French-Canadian mill town left the classroom to work in the factories.

My mother, the youngest, graduated from McIntosh Business College, a sister completed nursing school, and her four brothers parlayed their football-playing prowess into college scholarships. Their mother, Gemma, never did learn to read or write English, but when she later presented herself before the local judge to take the citizenship exam orally, he waived the formalities. "I know you, Mrs. Soldati. You raised a fine family. You are a great American."

My parents would eventually meet through the extended kinship ties that at that time connected Italian families throughout New England. The first Checchi-Soldati match was made when my father's maternal uncle married my mother's oldest sister—eventually, my father was his own brother-in-law!

My father finished college with a degree in chemistry, married my mother, and moved to Boston, where he joined the fledgling Food and Drug Administration (FDA) as a fish inspector on the Boston piers. There was remarkable esprit de corps in public service in those days. My father would forge lifelong friendships with a "band of brothers" comprised of fellow G-men scattered across the country. With geographic distance between them, they were nevertheless united in tracking down the bad guys who were scamming the public with unhealthy food and bogus drugs and medical devices.

My parents rented an apartment in Somerville, a densely populated, working-class community abutting the tough Charlestown neighborhood of Boston. I was born around the corner from our home, in

Somerville Hospital. Children with names like Maria and Tony and Sal and Vinnie spilled out into the streets from every floor of the distinctive triple-deckers in the neighborhood. Our social lives revolved around the close-knit families of first- or second-generation immigrants, who watched out for each other as the fathers went off to work in the blue-collar manufacturing industries still operating at the time in Boston and Cambridge.

In the hierarchy of the era, the best jobs were in the public sector. Court officers, firefighters, cops, bus and subway drivers, and utility workers were near the top of the neighborhood's socio-economic food chain. My father was a member of the "company man" generation of the Eisenhower years, one of the nomadic young professionals who would transform the potato fields of Long Island, the horse farms of Maryland, and the orange groves of California into suburbs to house their upwardly mobile families. Dad served among the largely unsung heroes of a unique and professional American civil service that helped lay the foundation for the unprecedented, meteoric, and still unmatched rise in national prosperity.

There was more security in public life and, for my father, more fulfillment. But for those in federal service, it was also a relatively rootless existence, as he was transferred often to pursue promotions in jurisdictions around the country. Before the beginning of my kindergarten year, our family moved to Kansas City, Missouri where my father assumed his first supervisory role with the FDA.

It is remarkable how we are formed by our early life experiences. Kansas City would mark the beginning of my training in leadership. During a music exercise in school, the teacher selected one of my classmates to lead our percussion band. Taller than the rest of us, he seemed more mature and authoritative as well when he guided us through the cacophony of banging and clanging that passes for harmony among five-year-olds. I recall, even at that early age, being acutely conscious of something distinctly different about our conductor: He had the cut of a leader, and I wanted to emulate him.

In the middle of my first-grade year, our peregrinations took us from the banks of the Missouri to the swamps of the Potomac, as we settled back east in Alexandria, Virginia. Enrolled in the local parochial school mid-semester, I was seated in the back of a class of nearly fifty students, every one of us subjected to the stern focus of Sister Mary Zita.

On my first day in this new school, we were given a math exercise, a series of simple addition problems presented horizontally, one figure following another in a straight line across the page. The alignment left me puzzled. I was used to tackling addition Missouri-style: vertically, one number atop another, the answer to be scribbled below.

I didn't understand what we were expected to do, so I did nothing. Sister Mary Zita took one look at my copybook and promptly delivered a monster whack to the back of my head. I burned with resentment and embarrassment. Then she added a healthy measure of insult to my already throbbing injury by making me stay after school, where my copybook, along with those of a few other unfortunate souls, was handed over to a small group of my fellow classmates to be corrected. Not surprisingly, they wielded their red pencils with abandon, clearly relishing the authority they now had license to exercise over the rest of us. Even at six, I didn't think it was right. My determination to be a leader was born.

Leaders, I observed, didn't get whacked. And neither did good students. They weren't left to the mercy of others; leaders would never allow themselves to be put in that position. The value of leadership was apparent, and so, too, was the inherent responsibility leadership required. With the unpleasantness of that first school day's experience foremost in my young mind, I resolved that if I ever had the opportunity to exercise power over others, I would never abuse it. I would treat others as I, myself, wished to be treated.

Could I have put all these emotions and convictions into words back then, at age six? Certainly not. But that's not important, because the lesson was real. My resolution was set. And this new mission—to lead, and to excel—would prove not only a good defense against foul-tempered nuns (whom I would endure for the next seven years), but also a strong foundation for achievement and success. By the close of that school year,

Sister Mary Zita was offering me accolades rather than the back of her hand. And I never again missed another math assignment.

At the end of the second grade, our peripatetic lifestyle and my father's impressive performance on behalf of the FDA necessitated another move, this time to Denver, Colorado. Six months later, it was back to the nation's capital, where we would finally settle. I had attended schools in four states in three years. But from the first grade forward, my commitment as a student and as a leader would be unchanged. I was elected president of every class from the fourth grade through high school.

THREE
Washington, DC, 1960s

Sometimes when our fights begin,
I think I'll let the Dragons win . . .
And then I think perhaps I won't,
Because they're Dragons, and I don't.

A. A. Milne

OUR FIRST HOME IN Maryland was a two-bedroom apartment, where I shared a room with my two younger sisters. Our youngest sister slept in my parents' room. Happily, the squeeze was soon relieved with a bit of help from the Catholic Church, which rented us a house at a discount on a property adjacent to Saint Michael's Church.

Growing up in the Washington, DC, suburbs at that time in a home headed by a rising civil servant guaranteed that you'd be deeply influenced by the city's events and public figures. Whereas early in the century, the figures who commanded the public imagination were the robber barons and captains of industry—men like John D. Rockefeller, Henry Ford, Andrew Carnegie, and Jay Gould—the men who actually ran government captured the attention of postwar baby boomers.

To the adolescents of the early 1960s, no public figure was more exciting than the young presidential candidate Senator John F. Kennedy of Massachusetts. His energy and charm made the American Dream seem attainable for every son and daughter of immigrants—especially the Catholic ones.

Kennedy's victory over Richard Nixon vindicated those hopes and unleashed a national faith in the power of government that approached evangelical zeal. When the newly sworn-in president summoned forth a New Frontier and asked every American to play a role, we younger Americans were already signed up and ready to go, in spirit at least, to the villages of Africa, Asia, and Latin America, as emissaries of American goodness, hope, and charity.

We were even on board to explore outer space. When the Russians sent a cosmonaut into the void, all the United States had accomplished was to put a small metal ball in orbit. It was a humiliating display of the disparity in capabilities between two rival countries. When President Kennedy challenged the country to look beyond the planet and to land a man on the Moon by the end of the decade, the country did exactly that. To a young boy intent on immunity from slap-happy nuns and self-serving contemporaries, this was *leadership*.

Kennedy forged a politics not only of hope, energy, and optimism, but of sacrifice and duty—virtues much in demand at a time of turmoil in domestic and international affairs. Government was important. We lived in perpetual fear of nuclear annihilation from the Russians, which peaked during the Cuban Missile Crisis. But the Washington of my youth was taking on much more than just the Russians. The country was also engaged in an internal struggle over legal apartheid. This battle was fought simultaneously in the American South and on the TVs in our living rooms, as riot-geared police with trained dogs and fire hoses attacked peaceful civil rights demonstrators. This wanton violence was particularly repulsive to families like ours who, as recent immigrants, readily identified with the aspirations of African Americans not only to win basic civil rights protections, but also to gain the respect of their fellow Americans for their contributions to the nation and their communities.

The decision to use federal troops to open up school doors across the South was admired in our household. We believed in equality as a matter of civic virtue and deplored discrimination as a doctrine of religious faith. But it was frankly a faith that had little visible impact on our daily lives. At that time, the Maryland suburbs were segregated de facto, as were many suburbs in the North. No African American families lived in our neighborhoods, and no African American children studied in our schools. It was not until I attended Catholic high school at Our Lady of Good Counsel, in Wheaton, Maryland, that I sat in a class with an African American student—and he was the only one in the entire school. And it was years later, as I traveled the South, that I came to appreciate the traditions and strength of Southern culture and its extraordinary capacity to adapt to changed times and transform the region into a focal point of national economic growth.

It was only through my frequent weekend bus rides into the District of Columbia that I remotely glimpsed the reality of the two Americas—separate and unequal—that the protesters were seeking to change: the dilapidated schools, playgrounds, and rowhouses of Northeast Washington. Then in the summer of 1963, as Washington lay gripped in a late-August heat wave, my father took me down to the National Mall for the March on Washington, the greatest civil rights demonstration in US history. There we heard the extraordinary leader Dr. Martin Luther King Jr. deliver his famous "I have a dream" speech.

My father was a federal civil servant, but above all, he was an American. Our presence that day was an expression of his belief in the power of democracy. I was only fifteen, but I felt the weight of the moment. The great turning of the tide of history, as Americans—black and white, Jew and Gentile—stood witness to the nation that we could be. In the wake of that march, President Kennedy, his brother Attorney General Robert F. Kennedy, and all of the federal government would be indelibly linked with the tide that intervened on the side of justice in Mississippi, Alabama, Georgia, and Louisiana. That movement would transform and redeem the South, as well as the rest of the country, fulfilling Lincoln's promise of a government of, by, and for all the people.

In my family, and among my peers in the DC suburbs, there was a profound belief in the promise of America. Working hard at school, playing halfback on Our Lady of Good Counsel's football team, participating in the dating rituals of the day—I took these all equally seriously, approaching every moment with the conviction that if I worked hard, played by the rules, and embraced my responsibilities, any sacrifices along the way would be rewarded and lead to something better.

I had been raised in a household headed by a man who exemplified public service at its best. I had witnessed firsthand the positive application of government action to keep us safe and free and to extend promised constitutional protections and opportunity to all people regardless of race, color, or creed. And in spite of that fateful November day when an assassin took the life of a president, I had watched government resume its commitment to civil rights and stand firm against the perceived continuing threat of our Communist adversaries. I, like many of my contemporaries, had clear ambition at the time: make the best grades to get into the best college, go to the best law school, make the law review—and maybe, just maybe, you could get a job in the Justice Department. That was America as I closed out my high school years. But it wasn't the America that greeted me upon my high school graduation. As the song said, the times, they were a-changin'.

My high school picture, 1966.

As I prepared to go to college, things were also changing perceptibly in the relationship between the American people and their government. By 1965, the pendulum of faith in activist government began to swing in the opposite direction. US involvement in Vietnam increased, and Americans began to question the purpose of a war in a place and on behalf of a regime with so little strategic value or connection to our own country.

I was approaching draft age and the warm embrace of a college defer-
ment as this growing conflict developed into a monster that would result
in over 60,000 American deaths, 250,000 American casualties, and dra-
goon several million conscripts from the ranks of young Americans under
the age of twenty-six. Vietnam engulfed a generation in a whirlwind that
would topple a president, set father against son, and permanently destroy
the faith of a generation in their political leadership.

As I looked toward the next stage of my life, it was Robert F.
Kennedy who best captured the spirit of unease that many people my
age felt about the direction America was heading. The senator from New
York had an edge and an attitude. And he seemed to possess tremendous
compassion for those in need, even while exhibiting zero tolerance for
those who couldn't—or wouldn't—recognize our mutual interests. He
challenged us to work together to heal social divisions and reestablish
the primacy of hope in households everywhere, from the impoverished
hollows of West Virginia coal country to the crumbling tenements of
Bedford-Stuyvesant. Kennedy's presidential campaign, which would be
launched during my sophomore year in college, was a direct assault on
two fronts: the Vietnam War policy of the Johnson administration, and
the nation's utter paralysis over the crisis of race relations.

Bobby Kennedy, like Dr. King, saw the two inextricably linked:
There could be no War on Poverty while we fought the war in Vietnam.
And whatever the merits of our commitment to the Domino Theory of
Communist expansion, it became apparent that we could not possibly
pursue a war abroad while we were so destructively divided at home.
Kennedy and King, of course, argued further that we were guilty of
moral failure, sending young men to fight while children starved at home,
but debates over guns or butter are never easily settled.

Bobby Kennedy earned extraordinary loyalty because he required
more than just moral commitment. He demanded action. And he took
action. While decrying welfare dependency, he helped inner-city residents develop new housing and jobs to get their neighbors off the dole.
He invoked the power—and the responsibility—of government to step in
and provide opportunity where none existed. "Have you ever told a coal

miner in West Virginia or Kentucky," he asked, "that what he needs is individual initiative to go out and get a job where there isn't any?"

He spoke movingly of the need to reach across the racial divide and view America as a single, powerful, cohesive nation, not one segregated into various and vaguely united individual nations of skin color. Bobby Kennedy even challenged apartheid directly in a speech in Cape Town, South Africa, where he defined the quintessentially American image of hope as a power that could bring all people closer to realizing their promise. "Each time a man stands up for an idea," he said, "or acts to improve the lot of others, or strikes out against injustice, he sends forth a tiny ripple of hope, and crossing each other from a million different centers of energy and daring, those ripples build a current which can sweep down the mightiest walls of oppression and resistance."

Less than two months later, in the violent aftermath of Dr. King's assassination, Bobby Kennedy could still invoke the mantra of hope to keep America's eyes on the promise of a better day. "But even now, there is cause for hope," he said. "Even now, the upheaval of the last few days is not the only aftermath of tragedy. Even now, citizens have proven that possibility still remains: for peaceful reconciliation, for a common effort by black and white to eliminate the other America of deprivation and want, and build a new America of justice and freedom."

Six weeks later, on my twentieth birthday, Bobby Kennedy would also fall victim to an assassin's bullet. In different ways, both he and Dr. King sought, as Bobby quoted Edith Hamilton, "to tame the savageness of man and to make gentle the life of the world."

Their passing left a void, diminishing the respect and confidence in American political leadership of a generation and bringing an end to America's political adolescence. Idealism died as my generation mourned its passing anesthetized by a cultural cocktail of sex, drugs, and rock 'n' roll.

FOUR
The Rhodes Scholar

Education has for its objective the formation of character.

Herbert Spencer

I MATRICULATED INTO AMHERST College in September 1966. My father's aspirations had been limited to the University of Maine, where he could pay in-state tuition. Thanks to his sacrifices, I could go anywhere my abilities would take me. With little parental experience upon which to rely, I had determined to go to the most selective school in the country. If it was "the most selective," it stood to reason (at least to my mind) that it must be the best. Amherst, a small all-male college in the Pioneer Valley of western Massachusetts, was a member of the "Little Three" Ivy League and the most selective (determined by the ratio of applications to acceptances) college in the country. I applied, was accepted early decision, and went without any thought as to whether this was the best environment for an action-oriented, private sector–directed, sheltered Catholic-school product of suburban Washington, DC. It would prove one of higher education's greatest mismatches.

I had blissfully marched off to college, a top student, a nearly-ten-yard-per-carry high school football halfback, the student government president, acknowledged Most Likely to Succeed, and squire to a stunning girlfriend (a finalist in the Miss USA Pageant). I was convinced that I would continue my record of achievement, take Amherst by storm, date all the most popular women at nearby Smith and Mount Holyoke Colleges, graduate Phi Beta Kappa, and culminate my college career at Oxford University as a Rhodes Scholar.

Instead, I passed on athletics, disdainful of what I considered a third-rate program (of course, one of my classmates, Doug Swift, would go on to be a star in the NFL as a starting linebacker for the undefeated Miami Dolphins Super Bowl team of 1972). The stunning girlfriend promptly dispatched me with a short but pointed Dear John letter (this was mercifully before text messaging). I lost all interest in my studies, removing the cellophane from my calculus textbook only the night before the final exam (and reaping a grade commensurate with my evening's mastery of the calculus). And I became a recluse.

Amherst was an amazing place with one of the most awe-inspiring teaching faculties in American higher education; it just wasn't for me. Six weeks into my freshman year, its legendary dean of admissions, Eugene Wilson, recruited me to go to Washington and speak to a convention of the National Association of College Admission Officers and High School Guidance Counselors. I had done a lot of speaking as a student leader, but my local roots were probably the deciding factor in my selection.

I delighted to address this convention of people at whose mercy I had been, as an aspiring college applicant, just the previous year. I got on quite a roll that day, and when I returned to Amherst, Dean Wilson gratefully suggested that I moonlight and tour the country as an ambassador for the college. I said that I had a better idea; he could help me transfer to some place that I belonged.

I asked him, "Why did you admit me?" Without hesitation, he responded, "I thought it would be an interesting experiment." I had to admit he had me there. The campus psychologist had once said, "Amherst is an interesting place; the person living next to you may be a complete psychotic and people will say, 'My, isn't he an interesting person?'" Based on this, I would fit right in. Also, the residual Calvinism that Amherst's early founders had infused into the ivy-covered walls had a certain "appeal" to a product of the Catholic-school premise that if it hurts, it must be good for you.

It did hurt, a lot, but I remained at Amherst for four years and graduated—without distinction. In the end, it was probably good that I was taken down a peg or two or three (hell, probably more), because in the depth of my self-induced misery, I found myself in the field of American Studies. The interdisciplinary inquiry into the evolution and development of America's unique culture would not only help me piece together the forces shaping my own identity, but would also help make sense of the chaos that was engulfing the country during the late 1960s.

I had originally been an Economics major and spent the better part of my freshman and sophomore years trudging though the required curriculum of theoretical macro- and microeconomics and statistical analysis without any great intellectual enthusiasm. I found economic modeling appealing as a way to conceptualize problems and would use it to great advantage throughout my career; but the field of theoretical economics was not personally satisfying. I dutifully showed up for classes but was absent from the extracurricular life of the college. I was sleepwalking through "the best years of my life," until two events blasted me out of my somnolence.

The first occurred during the summer after sophomore year. After working all day on a construction site, I went to the Silver Spring home of one of my best friends from high school, Bobby Rafferty. Bobby, a good student and quarterback of my high school varsity football team, had a spiritual side that I had always admired. Although he had won the starting varsity quarterback spot at his college, at the end of his freshman year he decided to enter the seminary and become a Catholic priest. I remember a letter that he sent me during our sophomore year: "I have found a deep sense of inner peace, but oh, how I miss the girls."

That evening, we took advantage of the long summer twilight hours at the local public golf course. With three holes to play, I was down by two, but somehow managed to best him in each of the last three holes and win the match. As I began to get into the backseat of his brother's

Volkswagen Bug, Bobby stopped me and said, "You won, big Al, you ride shotgun." Before I could respond, he squeezed into the backseat, giving me the place of honor in the front. Five minutes later, a car ran a stop sign at an intersection, flipping the Bug upside down and slamming the roof into a nearby telephone poll. Bobby was killed instantly, his neck broken by the impact, while I received only minor cuts and bruises.

The tragedy left me stunned, but also reflective: Why had I survived? Metaphysics didn't come naturally to a twenty-year-old, but I instinctively believed a better man had died and I had been spared—perhaps to one day become a better man myself and provide justification for my survival. I would ultimately find meaning in Bobby's death when, twenty-five years later, I donated a gymnasium to our old high school in his honor. I spoke at the dedication:

> Many people have considered Bobby's death a great tragedy and loss. But I would submit that it need not be viewed this way. By the tender age of nineteen, Bobby had lived life to its fullest and achieved an understanding of its meaning that few achieve even into their dotage. He figured it all out: It is not what you are born with, but what you do with it. It is not what you take, but what you give. It is not about the quantities that you attain, but the qualities. And what ultimately define a man are his relationships, with God and his fellow men. These are things that Bobby knew. These are things he taught me and all of us who knew him. These are the things we hope that countless Good Counsel students will learn as they use these facilities and hear the story about the boy for whom they are named. It is through these students, our children, and our children's children that Bobby will remain forever young and forever among us.

The summer of 1968 was a summer of discontent. Protests continued against the war, the cities raged, and the tattered remnants of idealism were hijacked by Mayor Richard Daley's Chicago policemen when they beat and tear-gassed demonstrators in Grant Park during the Democratic

National Convention. I was still an emotional basket case as sophomore year came to a close. But Bobby Rafferty's tragic death, his inner peace and spiritual commitment, gave me pause as I contemplated the waste that I had made of my two years at one of America's greatest educational institutions. I resolved to go back to school, put my nose to the proverbial grindstone, and try to figure out what I was meant to do.

Early in my junior year, a second jolt sprung me from my malaise for good. Professor Leo Marx taught a three-semester survey class in American Literature, so popular that he conducted his over-subscribed lectures in a 150-seat amphitheater (the entire college had only 1,200 students). He was a mesmerizing lecturer, but one day decided to do something "different" and asked for student volunteers to adopt the characters of Benjamin Franklin and T. S. Eliot and prepare to debate the political and cultural aesthetics of the American spirit.

Predictably, everyone in the class wanted to be the anglophile Eliot, the urbane Harvard expatriate, fashionably alienated, multilingual, virulently anti-immigrant, who had drowned his Missouri roots in the fog-shrouded waters of the Thames. Franklin, by contrast, was the crass American aphorist and ink-stained apologist for business and commercial interests. Predictably, I was the only volunteer for the creator of *Poor Richard's Almanack*.

I approached the assignment like an adventure, immersing myself in the practical literature of Franklin, preparing a defense of his straightforward vision of a society grounded in middle-class values with middle-class ambitions. The day before the debate, I made, as requested, a preliminary presentation to Professor Marx. Spreading my binder out in front of me, I proceeded to run through my arguments. As I built to the climax and turned the page, I realized that I had misplaced the conclusion. I froze, paralyzed in silence. Professor Marx looked at me and, with genuine concern, asked if I was sure that I was up to the task.

Exhaling, I explained with some emotion, "I used to be an articulate and engaging speaker, a leader among my peers, and a very outgoing person, but lately, I've had a pretty miserable run."

He looked at me, unsure whether to offer sympathy or a sedative.

I stared back. "But I assure you, I will be ready."

At the debate, I let rip. Like the impoverished Franklin the day he arrived in Philadelphia with nothing but a loaf of bread and a head full of notions, I had nothing to lose. I launched into a spirited defense of liberty founded on an even prosperity. I brought down the house and was even invited by Professor Marx to prepare an encore for the next class.

Unbeknownst to me, auditing the class was Barbara Ward, the wife of one of Amherst's most distinguished scholars, John William Ward, who had been a professor of English at Princeton University before changing venues and disciplines to teach at Amherst as a professor of History and American Studies.

Several weeks after the Eliot-Franklin debate, as luck would have it, I hitched a ride in Professor Ward's car en route to Northampton, where I was taking a course at Smith College. His wife, riding in the car with us, remarked kindly on my performance in Professor Marx's class, and Ward subsequently quizzed me during the ride about Franklin and my interest in the inventor-patriot, who turned out to be one of his favorite historical characters.

As a result of that trip, I would later become an American Studies major and, in my senior year, an Independent Scholar, free of formal classes, under the tutelage of John William Ward who, in spite of my dismal academic performance, would go on to be appointed president of the college. Professor Ward taught me to seek out and study the links between the literature of a particular period and the moral, economic, and political cultures of its time. Through the interplay between a distinct American culture and its institutions, I slowly came to see culture as an organic entity—societies and their institutions possessing, like human beings, life cycles and personalities. In this way, I came to better understand the antecedents of my own American identity.

Professor Ward was an extraordinary mentor. He encouraged my natural propensity to "think big," but also tried to keep me grounded, remarking on one of my more imaginative papers, "This may be genius—I'm really not sure—but I'm certainly not going to give you the benefit of the doubt—B!" Thanks to this remarkable man and several other extraordinary scholars and teachers who comprised Amherst's American Studies department, my intellectual compass was set not only for the remainder of my college years, but also for much of the thinking, reading, writing, and speaking that I would undertake over the subsequent decades. Because of these educators, and their unique ability to help me cultivate my talents and inquisitiveness, I immersed myself in those unique accidents of history and those diverse personalities and events that make up the American mosaic and contribute to render America the "world's indispensable nation."

At Amherst, one of the most powerful literary influences on my thinking was *The Education of Henry Adams*. The autobiography of the aristocratic historian examined the formative influences of modern western history through the metaphors of the Virgin and the Dynamo. In an argument suggesting the organic shape of culture, Adams presented Mother Mary as the driving force of the Middle Ages, the feminine ideal who inspired the greatest economic and architectural achievements of medieval Europe: cathedrals.

As Adams observed, these stone monuments to Mary were not only centers of devotion, but also repositories of learning and the locus of trade. Population centers rose and fell in the feudal ages depending on the ability of the local bishop to marshal the political and economic resources necessary to raise flying buttresses and commission windows of colored glass to shine the light of Heaven on the faces of awed churchgoers. Kings and queens were interred beneath their stone floors, a sepulchral reminder of the power vested in the holy pulpit.

The Industrial Revolution, Adams argued, overthrew the cult of the Virgin and replaced the Mother of Christ with the Dynamo, the electromagnetic deity of the Modern Age. Streetlamps, railroads, waterworks, and factories all rose in obeisance to the holy generator. A new spirit seized the nineteenth century and would utterly reshape the twentieth—nowhere more so than in America, which recognized in material advancement evidence of divine approval.

Here was a way of thinking that transcended the static limits of fact and category. It was as seductive as the Virgin and as powerful as the Dynamo. Intellectually, for me, it was like soaring: loosed from the bounds of gravity and seeing the great sweep of history from a vast height. Later, I would seek this heightened perspective when devising solutions to problems and designing strategies for both the private and public sectors.

Henry Adams, scion of America's first family, great-grandson of one president, grandson of another, found himself a displaced person in the vortex of America's evolving culture in the middle of the nineteenth century. Yet by the middle of the twentieth, someone like myself could be similarly displaced, a stranger in an estranged land, where millions of citizens marched in protest in the streets; volleys fired and felled students at once-bucolic universities like Kent State; self-styled "revolutionaries" occupied administrative buildings at nearby Columbia University and across the country; less fortunate men my own age became military conscripts, some of whom destroyed villages "to save them" and slaughtered defenseless women and children at My Lai; iconic leaders fell to assassins' bullets; urban fires raged; looters rampaged; a bunkered machine gun graced the front steps of our Capitol; common terms like "weatherman" and "panther" took on new meaning; and "Burn, baby, burn" became, for some, a new national anthem.

But this was America, or at least America at one moment in time: the end of the seventh decade of the twentieth century. Amid this chaos, there could be only one certainty: It would all change—quickly. The essence of the American experience is its dynamism. To truly appreciate what this country is all about, to live in and cope with this roller-coaster culture, you have to understand change, actively embrace it, and if you can, anticipate it. America! Love it—or leave it? I decided that I was all in—I loved it and looked forward to immersing myself fully in its dynamism.

The deeper I penetrated America's mysteries, the more I came to appreciate her founding principles. We are uniquely dedicated to a messy proposition: We all are equal and endowed with unalienable rights. So committed are we to the maintenance of individual freedom that we persist even while careening off the deep end, as we assuredly did during the decade that started when I first set foot at Amherst College, my inconvenient but necessary way station on my would-be journey to Oxford.

In the brave new world that I envisioned, Henry Adams was theoretically no more and no less American than the grandson of Italian immigrants. The essence of our nationality is forged in our pursuit of the horizon, such that the newly arrived immigrant, barely speaking English, searching for work in the lettuce fields of Watsonville, California, may be considered as American as the contented, passionless suburbanite seeking to shore up the past from the inexorable forces of the future.

What I learned from Henry Adams and John William Ward profoundly shaped not only my thinking, but also my career choices. Applying those lessons to the political economy, I recognized that our opportunity society is predicated on America possessing the most powerful economy on Earth, and that our upward mobility depends on having somewhere to go—a tangible destination in an expanding economy.

In that society, public service could be rendered not solely by public servants, but by private entrepreneurs who create jobs and wealth, and with their own hard work ensure that mobility is possible for the rest of us. These are the captains who conceive of, embark upon, and then underwrite the American voyage that transports us all to the ports of progress and the shores of prosperity.

I was certain now of the kind of leader I wished to become. And while Professor Ward had been a valuable guide, it was my father who had provided inspiration and caution.

Growing up, our material means were sufficient, if modest. But my father always told me I was wealthy. He said that you start out in life with an unblemished reputation. Your reputation, he maintained, was your precious natural resource—the one thing of enormous value with which we are each born, regardless of inherited station. It was paramount to your life's career—literally more important than everything else—that you preserve and protect your reputation.

Since my father was a careful and proper steward of his own reputation, he was accurately regarded as a man of intelligence, integrity, honesty, and hard work. He loved, provided for, and educated his family and took all of his responsibilities seriously. And when he wasn't working, he spent his free time with the wife he loved and the four children they raised together. I aspired to his work ethic, determined to build an equally happy home life, and hoped to earn a similarly sterling reputation.

There was, however, one element of my father's life that I was determined not to emulate: the incompatibility of his passion for public service and the crushing economic demands of raising and educating four enterprising children. He had risen through the ranks to become the number-three man at the FDA, but was forced to shelve his ambition to head up the agency in order to provide for me and my sisters. He left the government service he loved, and at which he had excelled, to join his older brother Vincent's consulting firm, based in Washington, DC. There, he built an enviable client list of America's top food, drug, and cosmetic companies. He earned a comfortable living, taking satisfaction from the regard in which he was held by his corporate clients and his ability to bring them into compliance with the safety and efficacy requirements that ultimately served the public. But he never again achieved that full measure of satisfaction that can come only from doing what one loves most.

I resolved never to be confronted with the choice between fulfillment and meeting my responsibilities. I had no desire to entertain such compromises in my life or career. I determined first to attain independence and economic security, and then to allow myself the luxury to pursue my dreams wherever they might take me.

And so I decided to write the opening chapters of my public life in the private sector.

FIVE
Selective Service

War is at best barbarism . . . Its glory is all moonshine. It is only those who have neither fired a shot not heard the shrieks and groans of the wounded who cry aloud for blood, for vengeance, for desolation. War is hell.

William Tecumseh Sherman

THE COLLEGE CLASS OF 1970 was generally acknowledged the most disaffected in American history. During our four years together, social mores had been turned upside down. "Parietal hours," which restricted members of the opposite sex to meeting only in common dormitory space a few hours each weekend, dissolved into an orgy of cohabitation and "free love." Drugs, hitherto an unspeakable vice restricted to small pockets of the urban underclass, became like smoking: ubiquitous, as students and faculty alike experimented with every synthetic and natural stimulant imaginable. The neatly defined Domino Theory, in those days more a strategic doctrine specifying that communism must be contained at all cost lest neighboring countries fall to it like dominoes, gave way to angry anti–Vietnam War protests and crass calls for President Lyndon Johnson to "pull out like your father should have." Chivalry and civility were dead. Cleanliness was no longer next to godliness, as formerly clean-cut freshmen men and women eschewed all semblance of grooming. Hair length became an emblem of movement rank and commitment. Respect for seniority and experience gave way to glorifying those who had neither. "Don't trust anyone over thirty" became contentious watchwords of a generation. The optimism of Buddy Holly and sentimentality of Elvis were replaced by the nihilism of the Doors and Led Zeppelin. We had happily entered the ivory tower, only to descend into the bowels of a gulag.

I was a displaced person looking forward to putting college and the 1960s in the rearview mirror, but first I had to deal with one last imperative: the draft. All men over eighteen were required to register with the Selective Service for possible induction into the armed forces. Deferments were available for a variety of arbitrary reasons for people like me, who had the good fortune to pursue higher education. As long as you stayed in school, you were "safe" for four years.

The unpopular Vietnam War was a voracious consumer of personnel, as troop levels reached nearly 600,000 at the height of a conflict that extended over the better part of a decade. The draft was accordingly the principal source of political discontent for my generation. When Richard Nixon commenced office as president in 1969, he instituted a lottery in which all registered men were entered. If your birthday corresponded with a "high" number in the draft (approximately 180–365), you were pretty much exempt depending ultimately on actual manpower needs. Those who drew lower numbers stood a good chance of being called. I drew 110.

PFC Checchi, 1970.

Very few of my contemporaries at Amherst served in the armed forces. Society's so-called "elite" were quite enterprising in mining deferments—one classmate was deemed by a sympathetic doctor "excessively sensitive to sunlight"! I was no hero and I thought the war a colossal mistake, but I was healthy. It seemed to me that there was a lot of luck in life, and you had to learn to accept the good with the bad. There was an opening in the nearby Springfield, Massachusetts, Marine Corps reserve unit, so I decided to defer graduation and enlist. I headed to basic training in Parris Island, South Carolina, as an infantry grunt in April 1970. Although these were not necessarily the best years of my life, they were no worse than the ones that I had spent at Amherst and would prove at least as enlightening.

I was older, better educated, and fitter than the average recruit; most were a shade over eighteen, physically out of shape, and undisciplined. Many chose the Marine Corps as an alternative to being drafted into the Army, and more than a few chose it over jail, as judges offered alternative sentences to young miscreants. Nearly all were regulars, meaning that when I returned home after the mandatory six months of basic and advanced infantry training, they would go off and do soldiering for real—most in Vietnam. They were impressive young Americans from all walks of life.

The Marine Corps would turn out to be the most extraordinary organization that I would encounter. I continue to be amazed by the ability of those drill instructors at Parris Island to shape up these young men, myself included, in a mere three months of basic training and create such unit identity and cohesion. I was more than thankful that I would not have to go to war, but if I ever had to, I would want one of those young Marines in a foxhole with me.

My military career would be undistinguished and uneventful, save one incident that would demonstrate a personal style of leadership and irreverence that even the vaunted Harvard Business School later would not be able to suppress. It was not in my nature to keep my mouth shut and go with the flow. I had been selected a Private First Class out of basic training—an honor that meant I would have some standing as we moved on to advanced infantry training at Camp Lejeune in North Carolina. There, I observed that the troop handlers lacked the skill and polish of the elite drill instructors of Parris Island. Although as a platoon leader I succeeded in having my troops complete their assignments ahead of everyone else, I was admonished because I didn't yell or use physical force with my men. "You have to put fear in the men and break some heads," I was told. Without hesitation I blurted, "Where would Napoleon Bonaparte be if he had to beat up his troops to conquer Western Europe?" The ensuing blow took the air out of my stomach and the wind out of my sails. Troop handlers, I learned, packed more wallop than nuns. I was summarily busted back to private, a well-deserved if inglorious end to my active military career.

After active duty in the Marine Corps, I had no interest in returning to a campus full of pampered intellectuals. I wanted to do something useful and moved into a halfway house in Springfield, Massachusetts, where I served as a counselor for troubled juveniles. I completed my independent study project—an incoherent attempt to fuse biological and cultural evolution into an explanation of the unique development of private American institutions—and in December 1970, Amherst College mercifully granted me a diploma.

SIX
The Nephew

The chief business of the American people is business.

Calvin Coolidge

IN CONTRAST TO THE disaffection I felt for college campus life, my introduction to the job market proved engaging and full of variety. Over the
ensuing two years I lived in DC, Cleveland, and Hollywood and did two
multiweek tours in the British Virgin Islands. I analyzed and ultimately
negotiated the merger of two institutional wholesale food houses, briefly
ran one, managed a sporting goods chain, and analyzed the acquisition
of a retailer of pianos and organs—all before my twenty-fourth birthday.
Now this was more like it!

My father had joined my uncle's economic consulting firm, Checchi
and Company, a premiere contractor to the US government's foreign
aid program. Checchi did feasibility work on economic growth projects
throughout the developing world, which in those days was pretty much
everywhere outside the United States and Western Europe. It was an elite
organization comprised largely of MBA graduates of the highest rank
from the most prestigious schools. As the company became more successful, it started doing consulting for the private sector, then began to
manage individual businesses under contract, and later started making

acquisitions and running businesses for its own account. By 1970, its nongovernment activities dwarfed its government operations, and it had evolved into a miniconglomerate, arguably too mini and too conglomerated, but one hell of a training ground for a recent college graduate.

I had worked at Checchi as an intern in the accounting department one summer. When I graduated college, Gary Wilson, one of Checchi's hard chargers, contacted me to see if I would be willing to do some analysis on a transaction merging two institutional wholesale food companies in Cleveland, Ohio. He was unsure how long the job would last and, in spite of my lack of experience, felt that he could train me to do the required basic financial analysis. This was the beginning of a long-term collaboration that would continue at Marriott Corporation, where he recruited me when I completed graduate school in the 1970s, resume at The Walt Disney Company, where I recruited him in the 1980s, and extend through the 1990s at Northwest Airlines, which we acquired together as partners.

Gary was a great mentor for me, in part because we were so different. What I came by naturally, almost instinctively, he had acquired and developed through persistence, discipline, and hard work. I will never forget the performance review of my first six months' work. "I view you as a prize rookie," he said. "You have all the moves—speed, agility, great instincts, but"—and he peered over his glasses—"you drop passes in practice."

He had it right. Without intervention I was destined to skim through life, probably with some success, but limited to relying on natural ability and personality—the proverbial charmer with "a shoeshine and a smile." But I never would have lived up to my potential or learned how to effect substantive institutional change. Gary taught me that there was no reward for style points, however hard you tried or well you played. You either closed the deal or you failed. There were no such things as circumstances beyond your control. Your job was to control circumstances. What really separated the winners from the also-rans was the indefinable ability to will things to happen. And finally, as Winston Churchill famously said, you "never, never, never give up."

Part of my training with Gary also involved negotiating. I learned the hard way that he was a master. My first day on the job, he asked what I thought he should pay me. As a young man, not wanting to seem pushy or immodest, I named some absurdly low sum, thinking he would raise it. "Done!" he said, leaving me stunned. Fortunately I was living at home, or I would have needed a second job just to make ends meet. However, forewarned is forearmed: After that, our annual salary negotiations were like battle scenes from *King Kong vs. Godzilla*. They were brutal, and I would take great delight every year in storming out of his office, prolonging the process for weeks, and generally making him miserable.

Soon after, I received another negotiating lesson in Cleveland, Ohio, where I had my first encounter with the Teamsters Union. There was some disagreement in the warehouse operation where I was working, and the union representative, who looked like a classic extra from *The Sopranos*, showed up at my office. He stated both the problem and his solution, and I responded: "Let's negotiate." He stared hard at me, let his coat jacket fall open so I could see the revolver strapped under his arm, and said, "Mr. Checchi, we do our negotiating in the streets." He thought he could intimidate a twenty-two-year-old kid who was wet behind the ears—and he was right! For once, I kept my big mouth shut and went along with the flow.

I completed two years of apprenticeship at Checchi and Company and the Gary Wilson School of Management. I had received excellent training and seemed to excel while gathering valuable experience. But the name CHECCHI on the door made me question how much my success was merely the result of nepotism—defined in *How to Succeed in Business Without Really Trying* as "when your nephew's a damn poop!" I also wanted to confirm the seemingly solitary convictions about the essential role of commerce that I had developed at Amherst, where a dissenting pre-med classmate had attached a quotation from Tacitus to my door: "He had talents equal to business, but aspired no higher."

I decided to seek answers on neutral ground at the Harvard Graduate School of Business (HBS), the reputed West Point of capitalism, or "a well-known eastern business school," as it puckishly referred to itself in its many faculty-developed case studies, the core of its unique pedagogy. I applied and was admitted to the MBA class commencing in September 1972.

At this point, some might question the apparent paucity of my academic record, since I so easily gained admission to such a selective school. While I had two unique years of experience, I was, as I would prove to be many times during my career, in the right place at the right time. My contemporaries were decidedly antibusiness and the top academic performers were applying to other professional schools, most notably law school. All three of my Amherst roommates, including future novelist Scott Turow, would graduate Phi Beta Kappa and go on to the Harvard Law School. Schools of business were left to sort over the remainders. People like yours truly, who had failed to distinguish themselves in college, were lucky that the radicalism of the 1960s had siphoned off the competition.

SEVEN

Harvard Business School

I shall be telling this with a sigh
Somewhere ages and ages hence:
Two roads diverged in a wood, and I—
I took the one less traveled by,
And that has made all the difference

Robert Frost

THE HARVARD BUSINESS SCHOOL was the tale of two years, a summer, and the best deal of my life.

Having made a hash of college, I had something to prove to myself the first year. Hopefully the promise that I had seemed to display in my younger years was more than just the flailing of a big fish in a small pond. I therefore applied myself the first year with a vengeance, attending classes, studying long into the night, and chalking up an impressive academic record including first-year honors, the first and most problematic rung up the ladder to Baker Scholar, a lifetime distinction awarded to graduates of the top 5 percent of the MBA class. I was even elected section representative, the equivalent of president of my class and a welcome blast from the past. With all that, I had quite a full social calendar as well. I was back—for a while at least.

Harvard Business School is a professional school. Everyone attends to prepare for a career in professional management at considerable personal and financial sacrifice. My class, comprised of approximately 750 people, was divided into ten sections, each one a distinct unit, the members taking all their classes together and sharing much of their extracurricular life. Each day consisted of three eighty-minute classes, in three separate academic disciplines, involving three separate cases, describing three separate companies or institutions. The first-year curriculum was comprised of classes not only in the basic disciplines of accounting, marketing, and finance, but equally important classes in managerial economics, organization and human behavior, environmental management, and strategy. Preparatory to each class, students were given specially crafted cases of thirty to sixty pages containing the background, competitive market, industry, and environmental information and research necessary to make a real decision that a real company had to face in the real world. It was as close to reality as a simulation could get. After an evening's preparation, in which you tried to crack the case, you tested out your analysis and conclusions with your section-mates in an amphitheater where the professor played the role of facilitator, drawing out analysis, posing questions, and engaging the class in active debate aimed at achieving some general consensus.

I loved and thrived in this proactive environment. I was enthralled by the potential for leadership, combined with the alchemy of professional management that took human and material resources and created value—something greater than the sum of its parts—in the pursuit of socially desired ends. It was something akin to releasing the power of the atom. Henry Adams would have loved it.

There was one departure from the three-class-a-day, fifteen-class-a-week ritual: the Written Analysis of Cases (WAC), a periodic assignment to write a case analysis. The case materials were distributed on Friday afternoons, with each student's written analysis to be deposited in a mail slot promptly by nine p.m. the following Saturday evening, at which time the slot would be locked. The cases were read and graded by readers, HBS staff assistants to the professors. My first WAC involved a company with a marketing problem. Instead of developing a marketing plan for the company's product as assigned, I concluded that the company would do better to sell itself to a competitor. I proceeded to draft an elaborate presentation to entice a buyer. This solution was apparently over the pay grade of the reader, who assigned me the equivalent of a C, later upgraded to an A by the bemused professor. I seemed to be wired differently than almost everyone else; some would later describe my apparently unorthodox approaches as "off the wall," but I prefer the infinitely less prejudicial "outside the box." Off the wall or outside the box, this kind of thinking would characterize my career.

The climax of any first year at the Harvard Business School is landing a good summer job. This is where you take advantage of all your sacrifice, hobnob with corporate recruiters, and land a tryout at some enterprise that may lead to the Promised Land: the offer of a full-time position upon graduation. The most prized jobs were consulting and investment banking. I chose to do something less traditional. I went to work in Menominee, Michigan, for the Enstrom Helicopter Corporation, owned by the famous trial lawyer F. Lee Bailey. Bailey was an acquaintance of Gary Wilson, who had visited his company and concluded that Enstrom needed someone to do a diagnostic of its ailments and assess its future. He recommended me.

I spent a glorious summer on the upper peninsula of Michigan and worked my behind off to good effect. I put in a new financial control system, refinanced the company's debt, persuaded a top advertising firm to invest sweat equity in a marketing program, generated a long-term strategic product development plan, and even designed the commercial argument for a government contracting case Bailey was litigating. At the end of the summer, Bailey hosted a company-wide event, awarded me a bonus that effectively doubled my earnings for the summer and covered the cost of my entire next year at school, and announced (fatefully and to my surprise) that I would continue to work for him in Boston throughout the school year.

Aside from the work, the relationship with F. Lee Bailey would be an education unto itself. It was my first contact with a brilliant litigator.

I was flying high one evening, when he decided to teach me a lesson. He quizzed me about some innocuous thing that I had done for the company, and then in rapid sequence asked me a series of follow-up questions. At each successive round of questions, I became more confused, until I literally no longer knew what I had done or what the truth was. I was a wreck. He then smiled at me and said, "You have now been through your first cross-examination."

Working with Bailey also exposed me to the diverse cast of characters connected professionally to him: Ernie Medina, the captain of the company involved in the My Lai massacre, and Billy Phillips, the crooked cop who turned state's evidence for the Knapp Commission on which *Serpico* is based, and who also served as consort of the Happy Hooker, Xaviera Hollander. Most memorable was Glenn Turner, the cleft-lipped, unborn calfskin–shod chairman and chief executive officer of Koscot Interplanetary Inc., who was under indictment for pyramid selling in his hundred-odd -COT subsidiaries, like MinkCot, which sold mink coats. Turner was such an exuberant marketer that during his trial for fraud, as he poured himself a glass of water from a carafe, he turned fully back toward me in the gallery, his eyes wide, and mouthed "*Watercot!*" I can safely say that no one at the Harvard Business School had a summer quite like mine.

When I returned in September to start the new academic year, I was burned out but committed to work for Bailey full-time. I didn't do a particularly good job for him, and I am ashamed to say I also reverted to my Amherst form and stopped attending classes, a major breach and dereliction of responsibility at an institution whose case method of teaching is so dependent upon student participation. I, of course, tumbled from near the academic top of my class to the bottom, as grading was largely based on class participation. Justice would be appropriately served years later, however, when I lost over $500 million—the bulk of my net worth—because I had failed to apply the fundamental tenets of diversification taught in a second-year investment management course that I had skipped.

The Checchi name would eventually be redeemed at HBS. My son, Adam, later demonstrated that in the Checchi family, the apple does not fall far from the tree, but rather into a different orchard. He attended HBS, earned distinction as a Baker Scholar, won the Loeb award, recognizing the outstanding finance student out of his 900-member class, and shaped up our family finances while developing and commercializing a unique technological platform for personal and institutional wealth management. I'd like to say that I inspired this dedication and achievement, but that accolade should go to another.

While my second year at HBS lacked distinction, it could not be described as a total loss, because at the end of the year, I made the best deal of my life. My sister had attended Dartmouth College her junior year as an exchange student with a young Californian named Kathryn Dean, who happened to be pursuing a Masters degree at Harvard in Spanish Literature while I was at HBS. My sister offered to set up a blind date with her friend during my first year. It was love at first sight—for me. She was beautiful, brilliant, warm, and generous and had a great sense of humor. About three months after our first date, I even persuaded her to go out with me again. We continued to see each other, commuting between Boston and Exeter, New Hampshire, where Kathy taught at Phillips Exeter Academy during my second year. One night on the telephone, graduation approaching, romantic devil that I am, thinking aloud, I concluded that we should get married. She laughed this off. The next afternoon, I called her and announced that I had told everyone.

"What?" she asked.

"That we're getting married."

"We're not getting married."

"We have to, because it would be too embarrassing for me to admit that we're not."

She was unconvinced—more like incredulous—so I borrowed my roommate's car, went up to Exeter, and begged and pleaded until she finally relented. We were married in Cambridge that June.

I had assured Kathy that we would make a great team because, among other things, we were complementary. I was big-picture-oriented, I told her, and she was into the details. However, six weeks into our marriage, she sat me down and asked, "Where exactly do the details end and the big picture start? Are you saving yourself for the really big ones, like should China invade Russia?" This precipitated some minor adjustments in my comportment. Not long after that, she declared that she would never have to divorce me; she could just have me committed. I made a few more corrections. When she finally concluded that I was prematurely eccentric, I really knew I had more work to do. After thirty-six years of marriage, I know that I am still not quite up to snuff, but whatever I have become and whatever I have achieved, I largely owe to her.

Kathy would eventually describe living with me as like sharing a table with the Mad Hatter. As soon as she got settled, I would shout "Change places!" and the next thing she knew, we would be moving on to some new adventure in a different city. We had bought a fixer-upper rowhouse in the South End of Boston when I decided that I had done as much at Enstrom as I could and it was time to take on something larger. My mentor Gary Wilson had moved to Marriott Corporation headquartered in a Maryland suburb of Washington, DC, and offered me a job, saying, "If you have learned anything at business school, you could have a field day here." I put down the phone and looked at the former Ms. Dean. "Change places!" And we were off to Washington, where my career had started. She would get a law degree from Georgetown University and practice as a tax attorney and I would attempt to climb the corporate ladder of a large company. How difficult could that be?

PART II

EIGHT
Marriott Corporation

Afoot and light-hearted I take to the open road,
Healthy, free, the world before me,
The long brown path before me leading wherever I choose.

Walt Whitman

I RETURNED TO WASHINGTON, DC, and arrived at Marriott Corporation in early 1975.

Unelected President Gerald Ford had recently discarded his infamous WIN button, backing down from his announced fight to "Whip Inflation Now" in order to take on the more immediate task of breathing life into a comatose economy. A self-described peanut farmer, Jimmy Carter, would succeed him in the White House, instead urging us to whip "malaise." Meanwhile, we waited in long lines on odd and even days of the month, just trying to put gasoline in our cars courtesy of the newly formed OPEC cartel. Casey Stengel could have asked of the US government what he did of the New York Mets: "Can anyone here play this game?" But this was no game, and the effects were real, as large employers like Marriott struggled to keep their people working and their heads above water. This period of economic stagnation, double-digit interest rates, and high inflation would persist throughout my entire career at Marriott.

The caliber of government leadership had deteriorated markedly since I had proudly worn my Kennedy button and dedicated professionals like my father manned the civil service. These were among the worst of times economically, and what Jimmy Carter took to be malaise was an unexpressed but widely felt lack of confidence in our public leadership.

Marriott in the 1970s was a tightly controlled, disciplined organization headed by a remarkable chief executive officer. Although his name was on the door and he was the son of the founder, J. W. "Bill" Marriott Jr. was certainly not a "damn poop." He had succeeded in business by really trying! He was a hard working, self-effacing, highly detail-oriented, courageous manager, the best kind of leader—one who led by example—and simply the best CEO I ever encountered. Responding to the difficult economic environment, Bill Marriott had declared a company-wide hiring freeze. Gary Wilson must have figured that as the company treasurer he had the authority to bring on board a lowly entry-level analyst, but when I arrived, his conviction seemed to waver. At Gary's insistence, to avoid detection, I spent my first two months bolting out of the employee cafeteria each time Bill Marriott appeared. If not mean, I would certainly be lean as I commenced perhaps the most productive seven years of my business career.

Marriott was one of America's largest and best-run companies, but it was running out of money—at least for expansion. Hotels were large, expensive "plants" that took many years to pay for themselves. In the American capital markets of the late 1970s, unlike today, there were no public instruments available for financing real estate. Each deal had to be separately pieced together. The larger projects required putting together several commercial banks to advance the funds during construction and a similar number of large insurance companies to replace the banks and issue long-term mortgages when construction was completed.

Similarly, most large corporations could not issue bonds to raise general corporate funds. In those days, only a very few (fewer than five hundred) companies in America could issue long-term bonds that, like home mortgages, had fixed interest rates and long ten- to twenty-year repayment terms—and Marriott was not one of them. Public debt was restricted only to those very large institutions like AT&T or General Electric that maintained the strictest and most conservative financial ratios. It was obvious that Marriott could not grow in the hotel business and simultaneously maintain these low debt levels. Shut out of the public bond market, Marriott had to rely on commercial bank loans with floating interest rates and short three- to five-year repayment terms. These placed severe limits on how much corporate debt it could raise and how much overall debt it could safely maintain.

When I arrived, Marriott was at the limits of its ability to borrow from banks. It had ambitions to expand beyond its staple of moderately priced suburban motor hotels and develop larger downtown convention-type properties. These were more expensive and particularly difficult to finance in the problematic economic environment of 1975, when interest rates reached double digits. Two very large projects, a hotel expansion in New Orleans and the development of a large new convention hotel in Chicago, were on hold. Marriott did not have the capacity to develop and own them, and no one had found an alternative way to proceed. Since failure was inevitable in the midst of recession, inflation, and high interest rates, and since I apparently was judged expendable, I was given the challenge of financing and developing what would be two of the largest real estate projects to be undertaken in America in the mid 1970s.

Six months earlier, during the first summer months of our marriage in Boston, as a recently minted MBA, I had calculated our household financial needs and confidently told Kathy that we would not need her to draw income until she began teaching again in September. Somehow, a week later, it became apparent that I had gotten the "details" wrong and, panic-stricken, told her that she had to go to work—immediately. This landed her in the "Banana War Room" of United Brands, where she spent the summer routing banana-laden freighters from South America. I, of course, quipped that this was a great opportunity for practicing her Spanish, but "Chiquita of Boston," as I dubbed her, was not amused. Now, after uprooting her to Washington, DC, I could not blow it again. For her sake, at least, I had to succeed, finance the hotels, and avoid losing the job I wasn't supposed to have in the first place.

I reasoned that since Marriott could not afford to carry the debt on financial statements that came from owning its hotels directly, the corporation would have to finance, develop, and control the projects, but have someone else at least *appear* to carry the debt. All I had to do was find debt holders willing to make the loans to Marriott nonrecourse—that is, base repayment solely on the hotels' performance, and piece together enough investors to make up a syndicate with 51 percent nominal ownership of the equity. This would allow Marriott's accounting firm, under current accounting rules, to let the huge debt float past Marriott's accounts and into the financial ether. Marriott would finance, develop, control, and manage the projects under long-term seventy-five-year contracts, providing it 3 percent of annual revenues and 20 percent of all cash generated (before paying for the debt). It also would receive in perpetuity 49 percent of the residual benefits as an owner. This formula and this approach, with subsequent variances and refinements, later accelerated Marriott's rate of hotel development from 600 rooms per year in 1975 to over 10,000 rooms five years later, and over the next thirty-five years enabled it to expand from fewer than twenty hotels to nearly 3,700 properties. This change would indeed prove transformational.

Unfortunately, there is an old adage that you have to spend money to make money. As I proceeded down the path of putting together the financing for these projects, Marriott had to spend millions of dollars in development costs. No institution would put up the construction funds or provide the necessary guaranteed funds at completion unless it was satisfied that all the architectural plans were complete, permits were in place, and outside equity (ownership) and other financial commitments were funded. If one piece of the transaction unraveled, all of it would, and each piece and each participant had their own time schedules and idiosyncrasies.

The process was nerve-wracking for all concerned. It was like inflating a large balloon. As it got larger and larger, it had the capacity to end in a bigger explosion. Failure of one piece would blow up the whole deal. I felt like the sorcerer's apprentice in Disney's *Fantasia*. As the process began taking on a life of its own, I became increasingly desperate. For example, the manager for the American Medical Association pension fund, one of the equity participants, was slated to sign a binding commitment. When our lawyers arrived as scheduled in Chicago to get his signature, his secretary claimed his plane has been delayed due to thunderstorms and he would be unable to meet. When our lawyers called me in a panic to report, I insisted, "No, he's in his office. Go in there and get him." They did. He was there, and in embarrassment, he signed. To this day I don't know how I knew he was in that office. At another scheduled signing that I attended personally, the young "salary man" representing Nichiman, a major Japanese trading company, was advised at the last minute by his American lawyers against committing to the deal. I stood up and said, "Who are you going to listen to, your lawyers or me?" And miraculously, he signed, too.

It took the work of an entire team to pull off these projects. When I needed help, I was given it—some better than other. Gary Wilson was an excellent manager, but his bedside manner often left something to be desired. He could be alternately imperious (Bill Marriott referred to him as "The Baron") and impervious (the head of the construction department dubbed him "The Armadillo"). Regardless, I was twenty-six-years-old, and I needed him for some of the heavy lifting. For example, I had trouble with the aristocratic, somewhat irascible lawyer of our partners in the New Orleans project and asked Gary to intercede. I don't recall what he said, but I do remember the conversation coming to an abrupt and loud end as the lawyer screamed over Gary's speakerphone, "And you can eat it with salt and pepper on it!" before slamming down the receiver. I looked at Gary and drily commented, "Thanks, that certainly went well." At one point, fairly early on, we were at a social event, and I was anxious to take the temperature of our potential Japanese partner. Gary took it upon himself to proceed across the room and chat with him. When he returned, I asked how it went. He said, "I don't know; he was a little hard to understand, but he smiled and took my picture!"

Nothing quite like these deals had been put together before—certainly not by me. I was young and balancing on an increasingly narrow ledge. I had put to use all that I had learned at home, at school, and in the workplace—some conscious and some instinctive. With a great deal of help and support, the projects were completed. At closing, I felt no joy, only relief. Thanks to those two deals, I would be a "made man" at Marriott. I had been terrified of failure. I had given it my all. I had exhibited some skill and pretty good instincts, but I also knew I was damned lucky. It could so easily have gone the other way.

And the hits kept coming.

Marriott was completing construction of a moderate-sized hotel in the Chicago suburbs. It was determined that we should try to sell it to a large institution, like an insurance company, and take back a contract to manage it as we had in Chicago and New Orleans—the difference being that this time, the investor would have to own it 100 percent. We made the sale, and it gave us some more breathing room. At least we could take the equity from the hotel that we had sold and put it into a new one, but financing hotels was still a tortuous one-off process.

It was tough enough to finance solid projects. I didn't fancy the prospect of trying to raise money for a turkey. For example, shortly after the closing of the New Orleans and Chicago projects, I was summoned to a meeting to discuss a hotel deal that Bill Marriott was really pushing. It involved converting an apartment building in Los Angeles to a hotel, and Bill wanted all hands from operations, marketing, architecture, construction, and finance to meet and finalize our commitment. As we sat in the meeting room awaiting Bill's arrival, the heads of the departments were unanimously grousing about what a terrible project it was—all for very good reasons, which they articulated. When Bill Marriott arrived, he clapped his hands together and asked, "How is my favorite hotel deal coming?" Each executive dutifully sang its praises. He looked at me and said, "You're awfully quiet, for a change—what do you think?" I said that I thought it was a lousy project and gave all the reasons that I had heard in the room before his arrival. He looked at me, frowned, exclaimed, "You're right, kill it!" and walked out of the room.

In addition to hotels, Marriott had extensive restaurant and institutional food-service operations, theme parks, and was the world's largest provider of airline in-flight catering. But the growth opportunities were in hotels—if you could afford to build them. Marriott owned about twenty hotels outright, and that was all they could afford at the time. It was evident that if we had to piece together the financing in advance for every individual project, as I had done in New Orleans and Chicago, we wouldn't be building too many more hotels. It was too difficult, with too many moving parts. We were lucky on those, but you can't build a business strategy based on luck (unless you are in the securities business, as I would later discover). We needed something new.

One afternoon, as we drove to a meeting, I was sitting in the backseat of the car behind Bill Marriott and Gary Wilson. I suddenly had an idea: "We could take a package of our old hotels and sell them below their accounting-book values, at their tax-book values, to avoid paying recapture taxes; structure management contracts at variable rates to produce a uniform yield to the institutional investors; and despite the investor returns, our reported profits would be higher for three years due to our having eliminated our noncash depreciation charges; so that by the time we had redeployed the cash and built more hotels, we would have uninterrupted growth in our earnings." If the reader doesn't understand this, it's okay. Bill Marriott understood what he had to: He could accelerate his hotel development program. But Gary Wilson was furious. After we returned to the office he lambasted me: "How do you know this? You haven't done any analysis." I said, "I don't have to; I know it works." However, like John William Ward, he was not about to give me the benefit of the doubt, and I would spend the next month in those pre-Excel days, doing the calculations by hand to prove that it would come out exactly as I had said. How did I know how the numbers would shake out? I was the grandson of Dina Checchi; numbers spoke to us.

I would go on to design and place this first package of hotels with the Equitable Life Assurance Society. In time, we sold nearly all of Marriott's owned hotels, built a large network of institutional relationships, and converted Marriott's hotels into an institutional financial commodity. I was promoted to corporate treasurer in 1978 and the following year also assumed responsibility for all Marriott hotel development, foreign and domestic. In effect, I was running the largest real-estate development and investment banking operation in the country. This gave me unique exposure to the many cities and diverse regions of the country—arguably the most interesting part of the job.

At any point, I might be managing up to one hundred open hotel projects in various stages of consideration and development. The hotels would no longer be viewed as fixed plants but as long-term securities, to be bought and sold as markets permitted. We could pursue our hotel development program unfettered by financing considerations. We could own and hold hotels and later sell them. We could sell hotels while they were under construction, or we could even sell hotels forward prior to groundbreaking for delivery at completion—even hotels with uncompleted architectural plans.

I can't exactly say that I was changed by my heady experiences at Marriott. More accurately, I came into my own. My values and certainly my personality traits had been established before I returned to Washington, DC.

I was still arguably a little "off the wall," but people indulged me because of the results. One day, Gary Wilson, who had become Marriott's chief financial officer, was chewing out our controller, Bill Shaw, because of some foreign exchange losses that had gone unmanaged. When Bill protested that this was my responsibility as treasurer, Gary dismissed him, saying, "You know Al doesn't get into details." On another occasion, in a fit of exuberance over a deal gone well, I burst into the office of our assistant treasurer, Peter Sterling, and did a wild fandango dance on his desk. He merely moved his papers to the side and kept on about his business.

At one point, I made a pitch to some outside investors in Marriott's new boardroom, where I excitedly used permanent marker to diagram my ideas. After the investors left, I was approached by Bill Marriott's driver: "Oh man," he said, "you wrote on the projection screen—ten demerits!" I had apparently wrecked the visual-aid system. Subsequently, I made a presentation in the same room for top management. The subject, "Corporate Financial Strategy," was of little interest to the operations-oriented Bill Marriott. Anticipating how long his focus would last, I timed perfectly his "need to make a phone call" with the entrance of a stunning young secretary bearing an envelope marked URGENT. Bill staggered back into his seat upon reading the message: "Just wanted to see if you are paying attention. —Al."

A few years later, in a tense meeting of his top managers, I took Bill through a presentation that would require him to make a "bet the company" decision. As he turned the page of the personal copy that I had prepared for him, he beheld a picture of himself taken at a Seattle hotel opening, sitting in a canoe floating in a swimming pool, wearing a Native American headdress. The caption read: "What? Me worry?"

During my term at Marriott, we made many strategic decisions. Strategic thinking is about making choices: examining what you are doing in response to changes in the environment and, where appropriate, establishing new priorities and limits. The strategic function, therefore, is among the most important of any well-run company and is generally directed personally by the CEO.

For example, Marriott Corporation had originated as a restaurant company, Hot Shoppes, Inc. Later, with the advent of commercial air travel, a new opportunity presented itself. What began as a small side-line—selling sandwiches and box lunches to passengers boarding flights at Washington National Airport—evolved into the world's largest airline catering business. Marriott's hotel business was relatively new. It had only entered the market twenty years earlier when it opened a motor hotel in suburban Virginia.

Despite the company's past success in the restaurant and airline industries, in response to unfavorable trends in these industries, we decided to change strategy and reallocate Marriott's resources: sell the restaurant and in-flight catering businesses and concentrate on pursuing our increasing prospects in the hotel business. Since the financial markets of the late 1970s made hotel ownership problematic, we redefined the terms of our participation in this industry. We ceased to be owners and became hotel managers and manufacturers—in the process creating new financial products for institutional investors.

At Marriott, some things were tried that never really worked out, such as the theme-park business. At considerable cost, Marriott had opened two the year that I arrived. By the time I left, we had decided to exit this business, too, and leave it to the pros like Walt Disney. Any well-run institution will have failures. To remain successful, you must respond to changes in the environment and try new things. If they don't work out or the environment changes, you evaluate and alter strategy accordingly.

Most people confuse strategy, the *what*, with tactic, the *how*. This appears particularly true in the public sector, where politicians have a difficult time making choices, and especially when those choices involve admitting a mistake or terminating a program because it is ineffective, obsolete, or no longer a priority. They would much prefer to add new programs or increase funding to an existing program, regardless of their results. That's why government keeps getting larger and taking on more with diminishing results. If, as Albert Einstein said, "the definition of insanity is doing the same thing over and over again and expecting different results," government is the place where the inmates run the asylum. Since private companies do not have the luxury of printing money or taxing, they have to make choices and respond to the dictates of the market and the limits of their resources.

In 1980, as Marriott saw more opportunities in lodging, we developed an entirely new product, Marriott Courtyards, designed for the midlevel extended-stay business traveler. Marriott subsequently branched out into every segment of the industry, including suites, resorts, the high-end Ritz Carlton chain, and the lower-end Residence Inns. Strategy boils down to two questions: *What are we doing that we shouldn't?* and *What should we be doing that we are not?* It takes discipline and humility to answer these objectively, and Bill Marriott had both.

Bill was extraordinarily indulgent, encouraging people to think outside the box, but he also maintained a clear vision of his organization's strengths, weaknesses, and capabilities. I, on the other hand, was always looking for the next big thing. Bill once asked me why I always had to hit home runs. I guess the answer was simply because I could. I wanted to buy United Airlines to gain control of their Western International hotel chain. I proposed buying CBS, which had fallen on hard times. I even thought of capitalizing a Marriott joint-venture subsidiary to establish what would have been one of the first buyout groups; I proposed using nonrecourse debt to leverage the cash flows of corporate acquisitions, as we had done in making our real estate investments. Buyout firms like Kohlberg Kravis & Roberts (KKR) would later do this and proliferate, charging an annual percentage of capital employed and taking a 20 percent interest in the profits, just as we had in our hotel-management contracts. Did Marriott therefore miss out on opportunities? Who is to say? It might have just been a diversion. Bill Marriott had a firm vision, and his company now operates nearly 3,700 hotels worldwide and is still growing.

In 1981 I structured my last and largest transaction at Marriott. The company that had been running out of cash in 1975 was now so flush that it was de-leveraging (paying down its debt). To maintain its stock value, Marriott would have to do something with all the cash that it was generating. It could pay large cash dividends (but these were not very tax-efficient), diversify beyond the hotel business into another business, or buy itself: repurchase its own shares (which we calculated were significantly undervalued) through a massive public buyback. This was the fateful "bet your company" decision that Bill Marriott made during the presentation where I had inserted that ridiculous picture of him in the canoe.

The analyses that I presented that afternoon suggested two alternatives: double the size of Marriott Corporation and buy The Walt Disney Company, or initiate what would amount to the largest share-buyback in American corporate history. In doing the share repurchase, Marriott would run counter to all the standing rules about maintaining conservative accounting ratios and engage in a transaction that would wipe out its accounting net worth, thereby taking the then-unorthodox position that what mattered was solely cash flow. If individual projects could be valued based on cash flow, so also should the whole corporation. Marriott had to be worth at least, and arguably more, than the sum of its parts.

Bill ultimately made the decision to buy back the shares. He was an operating man, and Marriott was a very well-run operation. He would invest in what he knew best: his own company. Now, all we had to do was figure out how to finance a company that was flying against all the financial conventions of the time. I reasoned that, since we had financed our hotel projects so that we didn't need to float bonds for corporate purposes, now that we did need bonds for corporate purposes, why not use hotels to finance them? I designed a corporate bond to be privately placed with our old friends at the Equitable; the proceeds would be used to repurchase the shares. Marriott would repay the bonds out of the future proceeds it received from developing new hotels and selling them to the real-estate investment arm of the Equitable. In essence, the bonds sold to the Equitable, nominally unsecured for Marriott, would be secured by the forward commitments of another arm of the Equitable. The Equitable would secure its own debt. This may sound complicated, but I'm confident my grandmother would have understood it. And after months of more laborious calculations, everyone else could understand it, too, and we did it.

There was no doubt that I had judged right about the public-service dimension of my chosen private-sector career. I took great pride as I looked about. Marriott didn't just build hotels, it built careers and created jobs that fed, clothed, and educated tens of thousands of families. A young person could start out working at the front desk, progress through many positions—food service, hospitality, marketing, operations, finance, etc.—and end up managing a major convention hotel, which was not unlike running a small city.

One of the rituals observed at hotel openings, and the reason that Bill Marriott found himself in that canoe in a swimming pool in Seattle, is the disposal of the hotel's front door key. Once opened, a hotel's doors never close. It is a twenty-four-hour-a-day operation that caters not only to individual and group travelers, but also local communities for weddings, bar mitzvahs, continuing education courses, fashion shows, Rotary Club events—you name it. Marriott was among the country's largest employers, and it was the nation's single largest employer of the handicapped.

I will never forget standing behind Bill Marriott in a kitchen and seeing the look of pride on the face of a young man with Down syndrome when Bill Marriott embraced him in a hug.

The Bill Marriotts, Sam Waltons, and Fred Smiths (founder of FedEx) are the kind of people who make this country great. They create the opportunities that are fundamental to maintaining our opportunity society. Occasionally, however, "when the team is up against it," as George Gipp famously said in *Knute Rockne, All American*, extra effort would be required to "win one for the Gipper." And the country was certainly up against it in 1980. We had slugged our way through a difficult economic environment, but we weren't making much progress. Then I saw that help was on the way. I attended the inauguration of the self-same actor who played the Gipper—a so-called "amiable dunce" who would reinstill pride in the American people, and help kickstart the greatest economic expansion in US history. He would also end the Communist threat that had plagued the world for over fifty years, triggering that misadventure in Southeast Asia that so affected my life and those of my contemporaries, not to mention the entire course of late-twentieth-century American history.

Ronald Wilson Reagan understood the value of the American character, of embracing the country's founding principles, of demonstrating courage, determination, and fidelity—all with a sense of humor. Based on the floundering of Reagan's immediate predecessors, pundits had argued that the job of the presidency was too big for any one man. Yet Reagan did it with ease, without ever missing his afternoon nap. The American economy quickly moved from stagflation into a historic period of expansion, and Ronald Reagan would go down as one of the twentieth century's most enduring transformational leaders.

During the Reagan years, Kathy and I would make another change, but not one inspired by the Mad Hatter. I was burned out. The hours were impossibly long, and it was affecting my personal life. My professional life was nothing but combat: not only negotiations with hundreds of individuals and institutions outside Marriott, but a constant struggle to sell my ideas inside Marriott. Large institutions, even ones as nimble as Marriott, don't change easily. Kathy's life was equally stressful. She was the first pregnant student in the history of the Georgetown University law school and gave birth to our son Adam on the last day of her second year. Despite the fact that Georgetown was a Catholic university, pregnancy was not deemed an excused absence, and she was forced to take her final exams as scheduled. I can still picture her in the hospital with our son Adam cradled in one arm and her tax notes in the other.

Despite our hectic professional pursuits, family was the center of our lives. We did not socialize. In 1981 Kathy became pregnant a third time, but twenty-eight weeks later she went into premature labor and our child was stillborn. We were devastated. I don't think the pressures of our jobs or our busy schedules had anything to do with the loss, but in the midst of our sorrow we began to reappraise our lives and concluded that we needed a change. We had been committed to building a future and made huge investments in deferring gratification, but our tanks were empty. We needed to slow down, regroup, and change pace and direction.

With Kathy's concurrence, I informed Bill Marriott that I would be wrapping up my unfinished projects at Marriott Corporation and would leave as soon as he could replace me. When I gave him my reasons, he offered to strip away my operating responsibilities and just let me "think." I was flattered, but told him that ultimately this would not be good for him or me. Culture was, I had learned, important. Marriott had a distinct one; it was a pure meritocracy. Everyone worked hard and pulled their own weight—no one more than Bill. It would not do to have one conspicuous exception. Besides, as I had demonstrated at Amherst, I was not wired to just "think." I had to be able to convert my thoughts into something tangible. I would have to move on.

About two months later, I received a telephone call, the same one that I had received annually for the past seven years. It was Richard Rainwater. I had first met Richard in 1975, when my efforts to find private investors for the New Orleans and Chicago hotel projects led me to the Bass family of Fort Worth, Texas. Richard was responsible for all of the family's nonoil investment activities, which were extensive and varied. In the pre-private-equity world of the late 1970s, the Basses were one of a small group of private individuals who had the capacity and the will to make direct equity investments in nonpublic vehicles. They were players, and Richard was their undisputed playmaker. He was brilliant, irreverent, decisive, spontaneous, and uniquely outspoken. Frank Wells, the president of Walt Disney, would later ask of him with genuine incredulity, "Richard, is there anything you think that you don't say?"

I had organized a tight presentation outlining the benefits of equity investment in my two hotel projects, particularly for noncorporate investors like the Basses. I thought that I was doing well when, midway through it, Richard stopped me and announced, "We can't do business together—you're as smart as I am! Why don't you join us and have some fun?" He was being modest. I was not as smart as he; I'm not sure that I ever met anyone who was. But, somewhat startled, I told him that I seemed to be having fun where I was and anyway had just gotten started and wasn't contemplating a change quite yet.

From that day forward, he always seemed to know where I was. I would receive a call from him every year for the next seven years. The conversation always started the same way: "Are you ready to come down and have some fun?"

When he called in late 1981, I allowed that, for the first time, maybe I was.

NINE
Texas Two-Step

Turn your face to the great West and there build up a home and fortune.

Horace Greeley

K ATHY AND I TOOK our time figuring out our next move. She wanted to leave the workforce to focus exclusively on developing our most valuable assets: our children. I, too, wanted to downshift so I would have more time with my family while I took my career in a different direction. I had three objectives, as I told Sid Bass in an interview: to diversify my experience beyond the lodging industry; to enhance and expand my reputation in the business community; and to achieve financial independence.

Affiliation with the Bass family offered the best prospects for achieving all three, but it necessitated a move to Fort Worth, Texas, which was alien territory to a Northeasterner and a southern Californian. The downtown building boom that was catapulting Dallas and Houston into the upper ranks of US cities had barely scratched the sunbaked ground of Fort Worth. As an urban landscape, it was not too far removed from its roots as the cow town proudly known as the place "where the West begins." Fort Worth was home to Billy Bob's Texas, the world's largest honky-tonk at 127,000 square feet. It could accommodate over 6,000 patrons and featured nearly every form of entertainment conceivable, including live bull-riding. On the outskirts of the city was a cowboy bar called Wet Willy's, whose sign proclaimed it was open "from sundown to fist fight." Early in the morning, as we gazed out at what served as the Fort Worth skyline and discussed the Bass opportunity, Kathy suggested that we close the curtains of our room to make the decision easier. We decided to change places and become Texans.

In short order, we grew to appreciate a unique state, where the Stars and Stripes shared equal billing with the Lone Star Flag. Texans are proud, independent, and patriotic. They are grounded by common sense, with little regard for the pretensions of the "pointy heads" in New York and Washington, DC. To my surprise, Texans and, as I learned, most Americans outside of the Northeast had little regard or interest in the antics of the self-anointed political and commercial elite of Washington and New York. We came to appreciate all the places that we lived: Boston, Washington, the Maryland and Virginia suburbs, Fort Worth, Los Angeles, and Minneapolis. The hotel business and my other activities took me to all fifty states and a large cross-section of America's cities and towns. To really know and appreciate the totality of America, one has to get out and around, and I was particularly fortunate to have been able to do this. But there certainly were regional peculiarities.

For example, one of our first tasks in moving to Fort Worth was to find a house. We would do a lot of house-hunting during our marriage, but nothing compared with Texas. As Kathy paraphrased Dorothy in the Land of Oz, we weren't in Kansas anymore. After seeing several places, we were finally able to make our real estate agent understand that we were looking for a home, not a natural history museum—several places being specially outfitted to display the occupant's vast hunting and fishing collections. We finally found a house that we liked. However, the title search revealed that it was encumbered in some tortuous transaction that even my grandmother wouldn't have been able to unravel. When I confronted the seller, he said, "Don't worry about that; it's just a little deal that I did because I had to do a little deal." We would find that Texans are addicted to deals. While much wealth accrued from transactions involving the development of real estate, the source of the largest fortunes was oil.

The original Bass family wealth was accumulated by a wildcatter named Sid Richardson, who borrowed forty dollars from his sister to "do some deals" and built a fortune in the Texas oil fields. Uncle Sid was a confirmed bachelor who observed that "women are like airplanes looking for a landing strip; and mine is fogged in." When he passed away in 1959, he left the bulk of his wealth to a charitable foundation and bequeathed the remainder and much of his oil operations to his nephew and partner, Perry Bass, and his four sons, who formed Bass Brothers Enterprises.

The Basses were not your typical Texas plungers. Perry and all four of his sons attended Yale University, with two getting MBAs at Stanford and one from the Wharton School at the University of Pennsylvania. I worked with Sid, the soft-spoken Savile Row–tailored eldest brother, and his understudy, the youngest brother, Lee. The second oldest, Ed, left the investing to Sid and pursued an interest in the arts, while the third brother, Bob, started his own very successful investment operation.

Sid Bass was a self-styled conservator of decorum, with a deep sense of fiduciary responsibility. His intention was to make certain that the Bass family interests would be deployed productively in partnership with people and in enterprises consistent with the family's reputation for discreet and honest dealings. This involved trying to keep some modicum of contact with and control over Richard Rainwater—no small task, as I would soon find out.

As incorporated entities, Bass Brothers Enterprises, Inc., and Marriott Corporation were similar artificial persons under the law, but that is where the resemblance ended. Marriott was a large, complex, highly structured and disciplined public entity with a tightly focused strategy. Bass Brothers was, to put it mildly, more free-form. Working with Richard Rainwater, I came to understand some of what I had put Kathy through; to me, he will always be the undisputed Mad Hatter.

Management and decision-making at Bass Brothers consisted of Richard scaring up an opportunity or developing an idea and more or less running it by Sid before he turned the matter over to others for the follow-through. Although no one ever said so, I supposed that I was brought in to provide skills and experience in negotiating, capital-raising, and real estate. That is, at least, my best Harvard Business School interpretation of my role. I would later take it upon myself to try to contribute some notional value of developing a long-term strategy for an operation that was opportunistic but unfocused. Noting that outside of the oil business, we were essentially a trading operation, I suggested that there would be value in becoming permanently invested in something large and self-perpetuating.

My first day on the job, Richard corralled me and said to stick close to him and help him "do the deals" because he was the one who made things happen. "Checchi, Checchi, Checchi, we're going to be rich, rich, rich," he repeated. I had nothing against money, but as a corporate guy, I wanted to know the really important thing: What title would I have? He said, "I don't know, whatever you want, but Sid has president." Sid then took me to lunch and said, "Try and keep an eye on Richard and keep me informed because I never know what he is doing." I would learn that this was by no means a question of trust between them. Richard was a faithful fiduciary and he was totally transparent. It's just that if you weren't literally sitting next to him, you had no idea what this free spirit would do next.

The Basses were an exceptionally philanthropic family. They had restored many of Fort Worth's historic buildings, built an upscale hotel, and opened a museum to house their extensive collection of the western art of Frederic Remington and Charles Russell. When I arrived, they were just completing a pair of thirty-story office towers that they hoped would anchor the redevelopment of downtown Fort Worth. These were ambitious projects that were intended to catapult Fort Worth into the fast-approaching twenty-first century, but the going was tough. Fort Worth had its own pace. One building was only 30 percent leased, while the other stood empty. Rainwater would quip, "The Basses are so rich they built an office building and a spare." When asked my thoughts as one who had developed and financed much real estate, I jokingly replied, "Do you have fire insurance?" Fortunately, I would soon have the opportunity to make more constructive contributions.

The first week that I arrived, Richard was selling a small investment that he had made in a company in Hawaii. He had received an acceptable offer that would net him and the Basses a tidy profit. He said, "You've negotiated a lot of deals. If you can get an increase in price, you can have ten percent of it." I increased the price by a third and earned myself a quick half-million dollars while giving Richard heart palpitations. "I don't ever want to watch you do that again," he said. I would subsequently negotiate quite a few sales for the Basses, but Richard would never again sit in the room. He was extraordinary at spotting profitable opportunities (far better than I was), but negotiating and putting complex transactions together is a whole different skill. It involves analyzing the other party's position, often helping them analyze it themselves, persuading them to take a chance and do something different, and having the confidence to risk the acceptable to get the optimal. This was what I had done hundreds of times at Marriott, and this was what I did at Bass Brothers. Richard and I were a great team. He would call the plays, and I would execute. He just hated to watch.

Since I would have to do the capital-raising at Bass Brothers, I thought a good place to start was to meet the bankers with whom they were already doing business. Opportunity presented itself when Kathy and I were invited to attend an outing sponsored by Morgan Guaranty Trust, one of the banks that serviced the Bass Oil Company. Morgan was the bluest of blue-chip banks of that time. When we were introduced to the New York–based vice president in charge of the Bass account, he looked at me and said, "So you're Al Checchi. You know, it's funny how you imagine someone whose name you read but you haven't seen them. I thought you would be fat and greasy." For once in my life, I was speechless. I couldn't tell if the Texans had it right and these Easterners were "pointy-headed" or just run-of-the-mill blockheads!

Much of what we did at Bass Brothers was highly celebrated, but I have to admit not nearly as complex or innovative as what we had done at Marriott. For me, it involved calling on the relationships that I had made at Marriott and applying the financing techniques that we developed for hotels to the acquisition of whole companies. As far as I was concerned, we weren't creating any value, only taking advantage of the fact that the valuations markets were putting on corporate properties had yet to keep pace with our hotel financing techniques.

When we repurchased Marriott's shares, we demonstrated that restricting a company to maintaining the low amounts of debt that the bond markets required was unnecessary. Static accounting ratios were irrelevant. What mattered was cash flow. Simply stated, could the hotel or the company throw off enough cash to pay back its debt? Public markets were slow to understand what would soon become the rationale for a whole new financial industry—private equity—and what would in turn drive the valuations of public companies, exemplified by the Dow Jones Industrial Average, from under 1,000 when I joined Bass Brothers in 1982 to over 14,000 twenty-five years later. Quite simply, back then we could make great deals at Bass Brothers because assets were cheap relative to what they cost to own. Also, we were basically the only game in town. The first major buyout firm, KKR, was at the time only four years old, having raised a mere $30 million in its first buyout fund. They would not acquire their first public company until 1984. For a brief shining moment, we were the one-eyed man in the land of the blind.

In 1982, for example, we bought a small subsidiary of a bankrupt company for $20 million. I was able to finance us out—borrow the entire purchase price nonrecourse as we did with our hotel deals. Our accountants said we needed to put something in the equity account, so I relented: We would put up $1,000. When we sold the property for $40 million a year later, *Forbes* magazine described in detail the transaction in which we "earned" $20 million after repaying the debt on our $1,000 investment—a 2-million-percent return. An acquaintance, Dick Blum, husband of Senator Dianne Feinstein, would later send me a note: "Good deal, Al. How did you raise the $1,000?"

One of my first actions at Bass was to compose a memorandum that suggested that the phenomena that we were experiencing would not last, and that there was great opportunity in buying certain public companies—either purchasing their stock, or taking them private in whole or in part, as we had done at Marriott. I listed twenty public companies of medium size that could be bought essentially with their own excess cash, in some cases supplemented by a small amount of easily raised nonre-course debt. While my secretary typed, Rainwater jumped up and down behind her saying, "Checchi, Checchi, Checchi. I've been here ten years and this is the first memo I've seen." I had not reckoned on the combusti-bility of arming Richard Rainwater with his first memo.

I expected that my writing would give rise to a discussion, and then if the idea was deemed meritorious, we would perform analysis to dis-tinguish among the twenty companies and the industries to determine which would make good investments and which, based on their specific future prospects, might not. Richard took the first company listed and immediately ordered Tommy Taylor to buy 5 percent of it in the pub-lic market. When the stock price fell over the ensuing weeks he hung a small doll with my name on it from the branch of a ficus tree in the trading room. There was a lot of good-natured ribbing. I even said to Sid Bass, "Stick with me and you'll be rich—right now you're very rich." But within five years, 75 percent of the companies on that list were taken private, yielding huge profits to investors. I would have to learn how to work with Richard. I never sent him another memo!

The acquisition and disposal of Arvida Corporation were examples of us getting it right—barely. Arvida was a large land-development com-pany owned by the Penn Central Railroad. It had huge tracts of raw land, housing developments, office parks, and golf courses in Florida (among them the TPC Stadium course with the famous island green). Penn Central was in the process of selling Arvida to an institutional buyer, the Metropolitan Life Insurance Company, for $280 million. Arvida manage-ment thought the price too low and didn't relish working for an insurance company. Management instead wanted to buy the company or at least part of it, but they didn't have the money. As I once had, they made the pilgrimage to Fort Worth, home of the Bass Brothers and the indomitable Richard Rainwater. When I heard that they could not scrape together more than a few million dollars among themselves and had exactly one week to produce iron-clad financial commitments to purchase this large complex company, I wrote them off as a lost cause and went home for the weekend. Richard stayed to talk.

The following Monday, I was in New York City at the headquarters of Merrill Lynch for a meeting with an investment banker. I excused myself and went to the restroom, where I found myself standing at a urinal next to Richard Rainwater. I said, "Aside from the obvious, what are you doing here?" He said, "I'm buying Arvida, and I'm here to raise the money." At that moment I understood exactly what Sid had meant about keeping an eye on Richard.

I don't think Richard had ever actually raised money in his career; he invested it. I told him that if he thought this was a good deal, it probably was. But, I continued, there was no way that Merrill Lynch, which at the time only put together small privately placed syndicates of real-estate investors like the ones I had assembled for the Chicago hotel deal, could finance this acquisition even if they had six months to do it, let alone a week. It would have to be done with a commercial bank. I called up friends at Bankers Trust, who had done much of the financing of my Marriott deals and had provided the financing for the infamous acquisition with the $1,000 equity. I explained the transaction, and they committed that afternoon to put up all the money, but they wanted 30 percent of the ownership. I declined. If Richard had been there, he would have had a heart attack. I then called a friend in San Francisco at Wells Fargo Bank. He took the red-eye flight east, and we cut a deal the next day. They would lend all $280 million nonrecourse on prime terms, with no participation in the equity. We agreed to put $20 million of cash into the company to increase its working capital and closed the acquisition within a few weeks.

Meanwhile, I had been following the performance of The Walt Disney Company ever since I had proposed acquiring it at Marriott. I saw Disney as massively undervalued and an easy fix, strategically. When I saw its stock price behaving peculiarly, I dared bring the subject up to Richard. I didn't want to end up in the ficus tree again, but something was going on with Walt Disney, and it bore taking a closer look. He didn't do anything, and a few weeks later, investor Saul Steinberg announced that he had purchased 5 percent of Walt Disney and was launching a takeover of the company.

Not long after this, I came into the office and was surprised to see Richard meeting with the chief executive officer of Arvida and his top executives. It had only been six months since we had acquired the company, and I couldn't imagine they were having problems. I inquired, and Richard informed me that he was selling Arvida to Walt Disney as a way of helping them ward off Saul Steinberg. In response to my question about the selling price, he said $100 million, which would give us a quick $80 million profit on our $20 million investment. I announced, "I'll sell it but I am going to ask for $300 million." I went to New York, accompanied by Sid Bass and the Arvida CEO, and we sold the company in exchange for $200 million of stock in Walt Disney. Within six years, that $20 million investment in the stock of Arvida, which we then exchanged for shares in Walt Disney, had a market value of over $2 billion. Richard and I, in our own fashion, had completed a successful collaboration. All I had to do was keep an eye on him.

The Disney saga was not over. Michael Milken, a young bond salesman, observed as I had that the American bond markets were not properly assessing and pricing risk. What the markets termed "junk," or below investment-grade, was generally of quality just as good as that which was termed "investment-grade." There was no reason that companies like Marriott should not be able to borrow money in the public bond markets. At Marriott, we were able to find an alternative means to grow, but many companies and many industries could not. Milken built a financial empire and an entire industry by making bond financing available to a wide assortment of companies and, in so doing, laid much of the foundation for the growth of the communications, entertainment, transportation, and many other major US industries. Today high-yield bonds are a major source of capital for financing the growth of a broad cross-section of American industry.

"Magic Mike" Milken liberated American capitalism, but he also unleashed its dark side. Capital is fungible. It can be put to productive use building things or, for less elevated purposes, liquidating or suffocating them. The 1980s saw a new species of capitalist gunslinger and extortionist: the corporate raider. He arose partially as a result of the new means of raising capital, but also as a legitimate response to a corporate executive class that had become self-serving and complacent.

Walt Disney had passed away in 1966, and the company's management, headed by his son-in-law Ron Miller, a former Rams football player, was uninspiring. Their watchwords were "What would Walt have done?" Walt had been gone nearly twenty years. Chances were he would have done things a lot differently then, but the Miller team was living in the past. The Disney franchise was accordingly in decline, its vast real-estate assets, film library, and creative capacities underutilized. It was weak, and it was vulnerable. Having warded off Saul Steinberg, Disney was soon under siege again—this time sequentially by investor Irv "The Liquidator" Jacobs, who I thought bore a startling resemblance to Libya's Muammar Kadafi, and then the arbitrageur Ivan Boesky, who was later indicted and convicted for insider trading. These, along with many other financiers, like Ron Perlman, Nelson Peltz, and Carl Icahn, made up the main cast of characters that assembled at the annual Drexel High-Yield Investment Conference, known as "The Predators' Ball." Mike Milken was a financial genius and an extraordinary salesman, but he was indiscriminate in who he financed, and this later became his undoing.

The raiders caused much heartburn among America's corporate elite, but the threat of takeover had beneficial effects. Many management teams and boards responded appropriately by reappraising what they were doing, trimming their operating costs, refocusing their strategies, and increasing the productivity of their assets in hopes of driving up their stock prices to full value. However, the private equity funds soon recognized the opportunity to move beyond investing in private companies and began offering to do "friendly" buyouts of public ones. While benign on the surface, many of these transactions merely served as financial windfalls for self-serving corporate managers and their enablers: investment and commercial banks, lawyers, accountants, and a host of consulting and other service providers.

Most public-company purchases were structured to give lucrative employment contracts and carried interests (free stock) to corporate managers. Many of these transactions were accomplished on a basis that significantly discounted the interests of the public shareholders. The resulting erosion of fiduciary responsibility demonstrated by self-serving managers has become systemic and a significant contributor to the dysfunction evident in many of our most important public and private institutions.

The Walt Disney Company, with our assistance, did find a better way. Roy Disney, son of Walt's brother, who had partnered with Walt in its founding, was a large shareholder, member of the board, and executive in the animation department. He recognized that the company had great underdeveloped value that could be realized by a change in management and strategy, rather than a change in ownership. We agreed. Aided by his lawyer, Stanley Gold, he began to push for a change in corporate control. We held several meetings and reached an agreement on their choices for management, and they agreed with our thoughts on strategy.

Peace was established in the Magic Kingdom when the Basses bought out the interests of the raiders Jacobs and Boesky, bringing our total holdings in Disney to over 20 percent. The Disney board agreed to reconstitute itself and bring in Michael Eisner, a film executive from Paramount Pictures, as chairman and chief executive officer, and Frank Wells, a lawyer and business manager with Warner Brothers, as president. We and the Disney family interests would profit the same way as all of Disney's other public shareholders: from the future appreciation of Walt Disney stock. Consistent with Sid's philosophy of doing only friendly transactions and maintaining a passive investment posture, we took no seats on the reconstituted Disney board and assured Messrs. Eisner and Wells that we would not interfere in management

So as they were just settling in during the fall of 1984 and Richard and I were paying them a courtesy call, it came as a surprise to them and to me when Richard suggested that I move out to California for six months and help them! Michael Eisner, of course, said this would be "great" (what else could he say to the holder of 20 percent of his company?). I tried to assure Michael that this was not preplanned (nothing with Richard ever was), that Sid Bass had not been consulted, and that he really did not have to agree to this unless he wanted the help. I am sure he took all of this with a grain of salt. I added further that if we did this, it would only be for six months, that I would give them my best advice, and then if they chose to ignore it, it would be between them and me, and I would not be reporting back to Sid or Richard. Under the circumstances, that was the best I could do.

Michael and Frank were accomplished entertainment executives, but neither had even run the divisions from which they came, let alone the entire company of which they were a part. They had not been exposed to corporate finance or strategy or the development of real estate that would figure heavily in the future of Walt Disney. I could help here, but I am sure this was not their first choice.

It appeared that Kathy was in for another move, but this time one instigated by the father of all Mad Hatters, Richard Rainwater. We would change places once again: from Fort Worth, Texas, the Checchis were going to *Hollywood*. With only six weeks of notice, we packed up the infant Kate, enrolled our two older children in a new school midyear, and made another move. I knew this would be a different experience when, a few days prior to departure, the morning before a huge testimonial dinner of farewell Bass was holding for me in Fort Worth, I had an argument with Frank Wells on the phone, which I ended with a huffy "Forget it; I'm not coming!" Frank had a way of taking an arbitrarily extreme position on an issue and challenging you to argue him back to your position. I had no desire to engage in this kind of unproductive exchange. I didn't have to. And I really was sincere: No one at Bass really cared if I went to California or not. Within minutes, I got my first taste of the Hollywood treatment. Michael Eisner called, described the situation as a terrible misunderstanding, and said that he saw me as the "Stephen Spielberg of corporate finance." He was really laying it on thick when I stopped him and murmured, "Michael, is this how you woo the stars?" I figured six months of this couldn't be all bad.

Hollywood is a different world. I had previously been unable to fly out to California to attend a birthday party for Eisner hosted by his friend Michael Ovitz, then head of the Creative Artists Agency (CAA) and often referred to as "the most powerful man in Hollywood." Instead, I had sent a bottle of fine wine from the year of Eisner's birth (1942). Eisner and Ovitz, whom I had never met, called me a few days later, and Ovitz proceeded to joke that for all Eisner knew about fine wines, he would have put the bottle in the refrigerator and made sangria out of it. I laughed and later sent Ovitz a case of Dom Pérignon champagne with a card: "To the Michael of discriminating taste." His return note of thanks, while correct, surprisingly lacked warmth or humor. Shortly after we arrived in California, I met Ovitz at Eisner's house and we hit it off immediately and later became close friends. I got it instantly: "You were wondering when the next shoe would drop and I would ask you for something." He allowed as this was the case. Welcome to Hollywood.

My contributions to Disney's resurgence were highly circumscribed. Based on my experience in the hotel business, I judged that Disney could build at least 20,000 hotel rooms on its own land that surrounded Disney World and massively increase the ticket prices at both Disney World in Florida and Disneyland in California. Location and competition were large factors in determining success in the hotel business. With a great location and limited competition for hotels and, by extension, theme parks, you had great freedom to set prices, the key to profitability.

When Walt Disney built Disneyland, he had bet the company on the investment in the park and bought only enough land in California to build it. Disneyland was highly successful and tens of thousands of hotel rooms, restaurants, and shopping outlets were developed around it by others who profited from Disney's investment. When he conceived Disney World, he bought over 25,000 acres of land in Florida with the idea of capitalizing on the similar opportunities that the park would provide. But Walt passed away in 1966, and his successors failed to take advantage of his vision. The result was that Disney owned 900 rather shabby rooms at Disney World and there was a several-mile-wide green belt of undeveloped Disney-owned land surrounding the park. Replicating the experience at Disneyland, developers built 80,000 hotel rooms outside the greenbelt, as well as restaurants and shopping outlets. This was a no-brainer for me. Disney could build all the hotel rooms it wanted on its own land and even "theme" them, and they would become the first choice of travelers. The same was true of other developments, such as shopping centers and restaurants.

In 1984, a ticket to Disneyland and Disney World cost ten dollars and there were 31 million visitors. Ticket price increases had lagged inflation, despite the fact that there was no competitive product in the world. The parks produced operating profits of $193 million, meaning that a one-dollar increase in prices would increase profits 16 percent. At Eisner's request, Disney management undertook a study to determine how much to increase the prices. I was riding in a car with Michael when he received the results: a ticket price increase of $1.75. I looked at Michael and said, "That's ridiculous, raise them five dollars." He agreed, increasing operating profits a whopping 80 percent with the stroke of a pen. Raising the ticket prices became the primary driving force of Disney's storied increase in profitability from the late 1980s through the 1990s. The average price is now over seventy-five dollars, and the operating profit of the parks has grown to approximately $1.3 billion.

Given that Disney shares were significantly undervalued for much the same reason that other real estate–based companies like Marriott were undervalued, I suggested that Disney also implement a major share repurchase program. They did, but when the price of Disney shares immediately doubled in response to some of the changes that new management was making, they decided to stop the program out of concern that the shares might be fully priced. I can't blame management for failing to foresee the effects of future theme-park price increases. The share price would increase over 1,000 percent over the next ten years. You can't always get it right.

Refinancing the theme parks presented another potential opportunity. I suggested that they might be sold like hotels, and Disney could manage them under contract. The investment bank Salomon Brothers had particular experience in real-estate finance and prepared a financial presentation for me and Frank Wells in New York City. When we arrived, we were ushered into a large conference room, where we were confronted by approximately twenty investment bankers, who proceeded to take us (page by page) through an approximately eighty-page presentation. My attention span exhausted after about five pages, I started flipping through the presentation. Interrupting the presenter midsentence, I asked, "Would you all look at this number on page twenty? And now look on page forty-one. If that number on page twenty is correct, then the other one is wrong, and this thing doesn't work." The meeting ended five minutes later. Frank loved it, and we bonded after that. Although Disney never did sell the US-based theme parks, it did adopt the role of manager in developing new parks in Japan and France.

Michael, Frank, and I survived our six months together. They even asked me to consider staying permanently to help execute the new financing and real estate development strategies. I had already done that type of work at Marriott. I had no interest in doing it again. Besides, I knew someone who could do it a lot better than I. Shortly after I returned to Fort Worth, Gary Wilson began work as Walt Disney's executive vice president of finance and administration. The team of Eisner, Wells, and Wilson would lay the foundation for the "Disney Decade," one of the great growth stories in American business history.

The one constant in all of American society is change. I had enjoyed professional success by observing change and finding ways to adapt to and anticipate it. I had participated actively in the process of producing change at two large American institutions, Marriott Corporation and The Walt Disney Company. In both cases, institutional change was evolutionary—new structures and new strategies evolving from what was in place. We didn't set out to make history. History made us. We took measured and discrete steps sequentially and responded to the dynamics of the economic environment.

However, once we departed the rarified and sheltered world of Hollywood and Beverly Hills and I made another visit to New York City, other changes and other realities intruded. As I rode into town in a private car, we stopped at a light and an old squeegee man splashed water on the windshield, attempting to wipe it clean with his filthy jacket. He was my dad's age, and the difference between my circumstances and his were startling. Later that afternoon, I noticed a homeless woman wheeling her belongings in a grocery cart along Park Avenue in Midtown, one of the tonier parts of New York City. The financial services industries were booming and New York City was experiencing a renaissance, yet here was another jarring contrast. On my return flight, I sat next to a college student. I asked what he wanted to do when he graduated, and he said he wanted to be an arbitrageur like Ivan Boesky. What had happened to wanting to work for the Justice Department or at least making goods and services of value to society? As my personal prosperity increased and I traveled in more affluent circles, I had clearly lost touch with what was happening in the wider society.

Recalling my stated objectives in that initial interview with Sid Bass, I realized that I had achieved all of them, and it was time to think about the next phase of my career and my other ambitions. I had developed more of a national reputation. I had even been included in a special edition of *Esquire* magazine devoted to "The Best of the New Generation: Men and Women Under Forty Who Are Changing America," receiving special recognition for my negotiating skills. I had achieved independent wealth. Totaling our "winnings" at Bass Brothers, we had made far more money than we would ever need. And I had diversified my experience base, just as I had hoped.

The Basses had been generous employers, and Richard Rainwater had certainly kept things interesting, but I missed being part of something large and complex. Staying at Disney would have been too much like trying to step into the same stream twice. I longed to move closer to my ultimate goal of affecting public policy. I felt that our major institutions were in decline. Many managers in the pursuit of personal gain had abandoned their roles as fiduciaries for the public's interests. Financial service institutions became parasitic on the interests of their clients. Hedge and private equity funds proliferated and speculation became rampant as they bid up the price of assets and took leveraged risks, much of it with the money of others. I had seen America lose its innocence in the 1960s. Now, in the 1980s, it seemed to be losing its soul. I was ready to do something that had more personal meaning.

Although I had been fortunate in my choice of employers, I had always worked for someone else. While this entailed subordinating my interests to another, it also enabled me to accumulate a diversity of experiences and skills and afforded me the opportunity to learn how to instigate change. However, I always seemed to have a wider perspective and a desire to pursue horizons different from my employers and coworkers. It seemed that I was an inveterate fixer—a problem solver. If I was in one company, I sought to change it and make it better. Looking beyond that, I wanted to impact the industry, and by further extension all industry, and then the country. Recognizing my restlessness, a friend once asked me what I really wanted to be when I grew up. I said that essentially I wanted to be a "secular evangelist"—in effect, to put myself in a position to articulate a vision of a better society and hopefully influence others to pursue it. I wasn't sure what form this might take or, more specifically, what I should do next to pursue this goal, but I didn't think I would find the answers in Fort Worth, Texas.

Kathy and I would have to change places once again.

TEN
The Wild Blue Yonder

If you want to hit a bird on the wing, you must have your will in focus, you must not be thinking about yourself . . . you must be living with your eye on that bird. Every achievement is a bird on the wing.

Oliver Wendell Homes

ONCE WE HAD DECIDED to leave Fort Worth, Kathy and I could have moved almost anywhere, but California was her home state, and I certainly owed her one. We had previously enjoyed our six-month term at Disney and had made some acquaintances in Los Angeles. California, for me, loomed large as the laboratory for America. It seemed always to be one step ahead of everyone else. So, California, here we came.

We arrived in June 1986 and settled on a house in Beverly Hills that was still under construction. I suggested that we spend the summer in Malibu. We were doing what I termed a "full Hollywood." Okay, *I* was; Kathy could not have cared less. My first day on the beach, I was lying on my back, enjoying the sun, when suddenly a cloud seemed to come over. I looked up and there was a six-foot blonde looming over me. It was a full eclipse of the actress Brigitte Nielsen, then wife of our next-door neighbor, Sylvester Stallone. I mention this only because it was the highlight of my summer. Malibu, I found, is seriously overrated. It is cold, isolated, and the beach is eroding—a fitting metaphor I would find for much of Hollywood.

In September, we moved into our new home, and I set up a small office where, over the next year and a half, I mostly read and thought. Some days, for variety, I would think and read. Truth be told, I wasn't doing much of anything. I was stumped as to what I wanted to do. I knew what I didn't want to do: I didn't want to get involved with anything that lacked the resources of a large institution and the latitude for action those resources would provide. I didn't want to work for someone else. And I wasn't interested in being a chief executive officer even of a large company. I had seen that job up close: You don't run the company, it runs you. I guess I would have wanted the CEO to work for me, and there didn't seem to be too many volunteers.

In February 1988, Kathy and I were guests of Citibank at the Winter Olympics in Calgary, Alberta. As the two dozen invited couples assembled in a guest cottage for cocktails, the front door opened to a powerfully built man, with distinct features, in his late forties. Accompanied by his wife, a dark-haired beauty, he paused in the doorway to survey the room, and our eyes met for a brief instance. This was my first contact with John Elliott, chairman and chief executive officer of Elders IXL, the second-largest company in Australia.

The Elliotts swept into the crowded room and were quickly absorbed. Kathy and I proceeded through the buffet line and found a small table in the corner. Moments later, we felt the presence of others at the table. Without looking up, I knew it was the man from the doorway. We plunged into conversation that must have been intense, because after about thirty minutes, his wife, Amanda, turned to Kathy and remarked, "I hope that we get along well, because our husbands seem to have fallen in love."

John Elliott is larger than life. Raised in Melbourne, Australia, he had cut his teeth with the management consulting firm McKinsey & Company, where he pieced together the buyout of a small manufacturer of jams. Through prodigious energy, superior intellect, and sheer force of personality, he transformed that jam company into Elders IXL, a

multibillion-dollar conglomerate with a near monopoly on wool trading and agricultural supply in Australia; ownership of Foster's Brewing
Company; and a worldwide merchant banking and investment business.
In addition, Elliott was president of Carlton, Melbourne's successful
football team; president of Australia's Liberal Party; and widely touted
as a possible future Prime Minister of Australia.

And we were in love, so to speak!

Perhaps what interested John in me, aside from our shared admiration for Winston Churchill, was his perception of my wasted potential.
He identified with me and simply could not accept that I wasn't involved
in some great undertaking, either public or private. In short, I had gotten
complacent, and he took it personally.

I will always be grateful to John. Through his encouragement, spon-
sorship, and great friendship, I gained exposure to much of the world
outside of the United States, met many diverse and interesting people,
and began to form a vision of how I could pursue my interests by acquiring an enterprise that had scale and international presence. We outlined
the structure for a new US-based merchant banking partnership between
Elders and myself. I would find one or more large opportunities to repurpose and build, and Elders would be an investor.

In October 1988, while I was still talking with Elders, I received a
call from my former mentor, Gary Wilson. In addition to his position at
Walt Disney, he served on the board of Northwest Airlines. Based on his
knowledge of the company, he thought that the board had lost confidence
in management, and might be interested in having someone that they
deemed qualified take control of the company and redirect it strategically.

As the full-time chief financial officer of Walt Disney, he would be
limited to using his private time to manage some of the analysis and
documentation of the agreements that this would entail. He wanted to
know if I would be willing to do the heavy lifting, putting together the
financing and an offer to buy the fourth-largest airline in the world. I
had recently turned forty, had a thousand square feet of office space, a
secretary, and an analyst (financial)—and I had flown on airplanes many
times. So, why not?

Actually, as Gary described Northwest, there were some similarities between it, Marriott, and Disney. Our experiences fit well with the company's perceived needs. Northwest, like Marriott and Disney, was a capital-intensive service business operating out of multiple locations and centered on the growing tourism industry. Sales and distributions were conducted through the same channels, and consumer segmentation was the same as the hotel industry. To grow, it would require that special combination of financial, organizational, selling, and personal skills to purchase and assemble a wide assortment of assets and link together disparate interest groups. These were challenges we had met before.

Most importantly, the airline industry had been consolidating over a period of decades and was poised for a final round of large combinations. If an airline's management could work through the regulatory constraints preventing international combinations, it could reshape the industry and would have a leg up on creating the industry leader. These were the kinds of challenges that Northwest's board did not feel its present management could meet. There was, however, one glaring difference between Northwest Airlines and both Marriott and Walt Disney: Northwest did not have a tradition of high-quality service. It was known as "Northworst" for good reason, as I would later find out.

Gary and I sealed our agreement with a handshake. We would be fifty-fifty partners without ever signing a contract. He resigned from the Northwest board to avoid any potential conflicts. The acquisition of Northwest Airlines would have to be friendly. But the potential hurdles blocking our goal were multiple and complex.

US airlines are quasi-public institutions, highly regulated by the federal government, which by statute passes judgment on the fitness of all potential airline operators. Additionally, network air carriers like Northwest engage powerful state and local interests, which can assert themselves to protect their sources of air transportation. Large international trade unions—in the case of Northwest, the Air Line Pilots Association (ALPA), the International Association of Machinists (IAM), and the International Brotherhood of Teamsters (IBT)—stand ready to paralyze the operations of any unacceptable party. A large capital-intensive company like Northwest also must maintain good relations with lenders, bond holders, and suppliers, or lose its vital access to credit. A lot of constituencies would have to be satisfied if we were to be deemed "acceptable."

Even assuming that we were wildly popular with everyone involved, acquiring Northwest would still require a lot of money. This would be no deal engineered to benefit self-serving management. The Northwest Board of Directors was highly independent and professional. They could be expected to negotiate the highest price possible. We would have to pay at least $3 billion to obtain ultimate shareholder approval for a change in control. Also, since the airline industry was highly cyclical, we would have to raise enough money on terms sufficiently flexible to weather the wide and varied fluctuations of the business cycle and myriad other factors affecting this volatile industry. This would be a defining professional challenge.

My marching orders were set. We had to show more management depth than our present combination of a moonlighting Walt Disney executive and an unemployed negotiator. And we would need enough money to support the highest possible purchase price, while allowing enough financial flexibility to deal with the unknown (this word later assumed new meaning for me and took on a life of its own). Fortunately, we knew a wealth of highly skilled and talented individuals upon whom we could draw as our plans developed.

Fred Malek had served as a senior executive with us at Marriott Corporation. The son of a truck driver, Fred had won appointment to West Point, served in Vietnam as an Army Ranger, graduated from Harvard Business School, worked with McKinsey & Company as a management consultant, and by his early thirties, earned his first million dollars in the buyout and turnaround of a small hand-tool company in South Carolina. He subsequently served in the Nixon administration in a number of capacities, including Deputy Director of the Office of Management and Budget (OMB). He joined Marriott Corporation in 1975 and headed, in rapid succession, its cruise ship, airline catering, and hotel divisions. Fred gave our group much-needed management credibility. Now we were three.

Bob Friedman, partner in Simpson Thacher & Bartlett LLP, managed all of the contracts, government filings, loan documents, and so on that an acquisition of this complexity required. My close friend, Friedman was the trusted lawyer who had helped me through nearly every significant transaction of my business career. He drew up General Partnership papers, and on November 21, 1988, Wings Partners was formed with approximately $3 million of committed capital. We arranged an additional working capital loan from my friends at Wells Fargo, who had financed the acquisition of Arvida Corporation that had led to the investment in Walt Disney.

It was evident that if we were to be taken seriously by the Northwest board, we would have to show more financial substance and demonstrate that we had "skin in the game." Five percent is the maximum amount of stock in a public company that anyone can buy before triggering the requirement to make a public filing. By staying below this threshold we would allow the Northwest board maximum discretion. They could review our proposal without any public notice or pressure. If they rejected it, no one would know that it had been made. If we were to have any chance of success, we would have to be friendly in the truest sense of the word. We decided to purchase 4.9 percent of the company before approaching the board.

To buy the stock we needed about $75 million. Although we had not finalized our merchant banking partnership, I approached John Elliott. This was exactly the kind of investment we had in mind. Elders was in, and we had our fourth partner. We started acquiring the Northwest stock.

Looking ahead, to put together an acquisition proposal, we would need to show the ability to finance it. It seemed logical to approach Bankers Trust Company, which had played a key role in most of my large transactions at Marriott, Bass Brothers, and Walt Disney—besides, no one there had ever called me fat and greasy!

The industry was in flux; the traditional divisions between commercial banks and investment banks were breaking down. Aggressive

commercial banks like Bankers Trust were moving rapidly into investment banking and using their own capital to make equity investments,
in addition to traditional commercial loans. Acquiring Northwest would
require significant institutional equity. We would also need a large bank
to play the role of lead lender—in this case loaning up to $500 million
itself and assembling a syndicate of up to one hundred banks to raise
approximately $3 billion more. The key to deal-making is to find a way
for all participants to achieve their objectives. Bankers Trust was eager to
play the main role in a large transaction and demonstrate to the financial
community its expanded capabilities as equity investor, financial advisor, and major loan syndicator. We reached agreement and they signed
aboard. Now we were five.

By mid-January 1989, we were well on our way to accumulating
our 4.9-percent stake in Northwest Airlines. Completing this nearly
$75-million investment would, we thought, evidence seriousness of pur-
pose. Our group now included three reasonably well-regarded corporate
executives, including one known personally by the Northwest Board of
Directors. We had added a major money-center bank, not only to syndicate an acquisition loan but to make its largest equity investment ever, as
well as a major off-shore corporate partner with a significant merchant
banking operation in the Pacific Rim, where Northwest had significant
operations. In Bob Friedman, we had retained one of Wall Street's most
experienced corporate lawyers, backed by one of the country's most
respected corporate law firms. We had made a good start in building a
team, but there were many more additions to come.

It was customary in public transactions to engage one or more investment banks. Every substantial transaction had at least one and often
many. We decided that we needed one, too, but not to analyze, structure,
finance, or negotiate a deal. We could perform these functions ourselves.
We would need advice on all the technical aspects involving the Securities
and Exchange Commission (SEC) and other agencies when acquiring a
public company. It would help to have someone on our side of the table
who knew all the usual suspects sitting on the other side, once Northwest
brought in its team of advisors. More than anything, since we were not

known quantities in the acquisition game, we wanted a big-name financial advisor for appearance's sake to enhance our credibility.

Accordingly, in mid-January 1989, we retained the firm of Wasserstein Perella & Co., Wall Street's premier financial advisory firm. In addition to their technical expertise and the credibility they added to our group, Wasserstein Perella would be "conflicted out" (that is, unable to work for any potential competitors). When other bidders later sought to participate in the Northwest auction, they would learn that we had "swept the street," and effectively tied up the top banks, law and accounting firms, financial advisors, technical airline consultants, and other service providers required to mount a complex professional bid. This proved a tactical advantage for us.

By early February, we were ready. We had acquired our stake in Northwest, and on February 13, 1989, according to a carefully constructed script, Gary Wilson called Stephen Rothmeier, chairman and chief executive officer of Northwest Airlines.

Gary informed Rothmeier that we had assembled a group that had purchased 4.9 percent of the company. We requested an opportunity to meet with the Northwest board to make a presentation of our capabilities and plans. Our intentions were friendly. We would make no offer requiring public disclosure and would not proceed further unless by invitation of the board. Rothmeier was appropriately noncommittal and said that he would get back after consulting with his board.

As expected, Northwest retained outside counsel and an investment banker. After several weeks of inconclusive discussions with Northwest's advisors, we received a letter on March 28, 1989:

> The Board of Directors of NWA Inc. has carefully considered your group's interest in exploring the possibility of a negotiated acquisition of the Company. The Board has concluded that the interests of the Company, its shareholders, employees, and customers will be best served by maintaining the Company as an independent entity. Consequently, the Company does not intend to pursue your indication of interest.

The letter went on to say, parenthetically, that the board had adopted a shareholder rights plan, commonly referred to as a "poison pill" (a legal stratagem designed to make an unfriendly bid more expensive and difficult). It noted that this "has been under consideration for a substantial period of time" and "is not expressly intended to be a response to your interest in the company."

We had discreetly proposed a transaction and the board had spoken. It was not interested in pursuing our proposal. The shareholder rights plan was irrelevant to us. We would only do a friendly deal.

We were crestfallen. Our six-month quest to acquire Northwest Airlines was over before it started. We regretfully notified our partners, and the following day we began quietly liquidating our common stock holdings in Northwest Airlines. We just hoped that we could sell the shares without taking a loss.

Unbeknownst to us, however, when Northwest arbitrarily decided to impose its shareholder rights plan, it was advised by its counsel that it must disclose publicly that it had been approached by a group that owned 4.9 percent of the company's common stock, and that interest had been expressed in pursuing an acquisition. Without imposing the rights plan, NWA would have been under no obligation to disclose such an approach. This public announcement was akin to waving a red cape in front of a bull or ringing the dinner bell in shark-infested waters.

The announcement instantly gave rise to intense press speculation about the identity of the 4.9-percent holder: Carl Icahn, who had bought bankrupt TWA; Coniston Partners, which had made a large investment in United Airlines; Minnesota investor Irwin Jacobs; oil tycoon Marvin Davis; the Bass Brothers of Fort Worth; former Secretary of the Treasury William Simon; the wealthy Pritzker family of Chicago; and American Airlines were among the suspects. We, of course, weren't on anybody's radar.

Two days later, on March 30, perhaps smelling blood, billionaire Marvin Davis delivered a formal bid to the Northwest Airlines Board. He offered ninety dollars a share in cash for 100 percent of the company's common stock.

Northwest Airlines was in play.

Marvin Davis was a large, heavy-set man with a gravelly voice accented by his native Brooklyn. He was a controversial character, but on one thing everyone agreed: he knew how to make money. Davis had made a fortune as an oil wildcatter and sold most of his holdings at the top of the market. He had bought and sold many major real-estate projects at huge profits. Most telling, he had made hundreds of millions of dollars buying large common stock positions in public companies, putting them in play, and then selling out to a higher bidder.

Northwest management, employees, and the Minnesota political establishment were horrified; we were relieved and thrilled. The price of Northwest stock soared on Davis's offer. Not only would we profit from our Northwest investment, we were back in the hunt.

Reaction to Davis's bid was instantaneous and negative. Guy Cook of the IAM spoke for labor when he protested, "If he has intent to do a leveraged buyout, or to take apart the company . . . we'll try to do everything we can to make those assets worthless." Minnesota Governor Rudy Perpich declared "war" against Davis. Other Minnesota officials joined with the governor in calling for the passage of antitakeover legislation and expressed concern "not only with the jobs of the 15,000 employees in Minnesota, but the 70,000 additional Minnesotans who benefit from the fact that the Twin Cities is a national and international hub."

A week later, on April 7, the Northwest board flatly rejected Davis's bid. Davis, true to his rough-and-tumble reputation, would not be deterred. A few days later, he announced his intent to wage a proxy fight to take control of the NWA board.

Speculation continued over the identity of the 4.9-percent holder until April 12, when an enterprising *Wall Street Journal* reporter, Randall Smith, wrote a story identifying Gary and me. The next day, the Minnesota *Star Tribune* reported high praise from Wall Street over our financial acumen, speculated that we would have easy access to money, and predicted that we might emerge as the leading bidder. Clearly someone from Northwest was talking.

Smith learned and duly reported that we had hired Wasserstein

Perella & Co. and saw this as a sign that we were "serious." I had to smile when I read this. Mike Hamilton, a securities analyst with Piper, Jaffray & Hopwood in Minnesota said of us, "The fact that they haven't shown up gives credibility to the idea they're trying to work out something friendly." Robert Joedicke, the airline analyst for Lehman Brothers said, "The real key is what the Checchi group is going to do. Just because they aren't visible doesn't mean they've gone away. They're sitting there playing chess, and they've got a very definite game plan. We just don't know what it is."

Actually, I was biting my fingernails, and I wanted to throttle Gary for getting me into this. Northwest stock was now trading at $97.25 per share, well above our average cost of about sixty dollars. The Street had spoken. In the hands of people who knew what to do with it, NWA would be worth well over $100 per share. We were going to need more money.

We began to receive numerous expressions of interest to help finance us. Most were financial institutions with money but little else. We wanted partners who had skills, relationships, and institutional capacities beyond money to help us build NWA in the event that our bid was successful.

Then we received a call from Richard Blum. Gary and I had known Dick Blum about as long as we had known each other. He had been a partner with Sutro & Co., a California-based investment bank, when he joined the board of Checchi and Company, where Gary and I had started out together. He had broad experience in corporate finance, had many contacts in Asia, and had established his own private equity fund. Dick was married to Dianne Feinstein, the former mayor of San Francisco, who subsequently became a US senator from California. Blum's fund committed $100 million to our effort. Now we were six.

By late April, Northwest was the dominant news story in international aviation. It was one of only three airlines in the world with significant legal authority to fly between the United States and Japan, and beyond Japan to much of the Far East (Japan Airlines and United Airlines were the other two).

International aviation is highly regulated. International route authority is granted only by treaties negotiated as part of the foreign and industrial policy of sovereign governments. Nearly all route authority is bilateral, meaning it involves agreements only between two countries. A US carrier, for example, will receive authority to fly to a country, but it cannot fly from that country to another. It can only fly directly back to the United States The agreements have other restrictions. They are airline-specific, stating which airline can fly to which specific city in the country, how often (the frequency), and indeed to what specific airport in that city, if there are more than two. And a carrier can never fly beyond its destination to another city in the same country. It must always fly home.

If assembling international route authority is like playing Monopoly, then Northwest Airlines, with its agreements with Japan and other countries in the Far East, had hotels on Boardwalk and Park Place.

The most valuable international air route authority was between Japan and the United States. Japan–United States travel constituted the vast majority of trans-Pacific air traffic and was the fastest-growing passenger and freight market in the world. Based on massive treaty authority dating back to the postwar 1950s, Northwest Airlines had the authority to fly to Tokyo from virtually every major city in the United States. Uniquely, there were no frequency limitations imposed on Northwest, other than those required by the physical capacity constraint of Tokyo's Narita airport.

Further, Northwest had valuable "fifth freedom" rights, also known as "beyond" rights, out of Japan, meaning it could fly *beyond* Tokyo to other Asian countries and from those countries back to Tokyo. This allowed Northwest to set up a hub in Tokyo and from there serve China, Taiwan, Hong Kong, Thailand, Singapore, Korea, and the Philippines. Of all the other air carriers in the world, only United Airlines had anything remotely approaching Northwest's Pacific route authority.

It had long been the dream of international aviation planners one day to create a single seamless airline system capable of taking passengers all over the world. This degree of integration was presently impossible due to the existing treaty limitations governing international aviation. But clearly Northwest's Pacific route authority gave it a leg up on other carriers seeking to build a worldwide system. Individual airlines had begun to experiment with a series of marketing and operating relationships to create a degree of shared consumer identity, cost synergies, and passenger referral or "feed." But these so-called alliances were highly restricted by regulators and were in their infancy in April 1989, when Northwest was making headlines.

Netherlands-based KLM Royal Dutch Airlines had a small home market. Yet throughout history, Dutch businessmen have overcome the disadvantages of their small domestic market. Through skill, determination, and prudent risk-taking, they have pursued world trade and built some of the world's largest and most successful companies. In April 1989, KLM was one of the world's largest passenger and freight carriers, and its management clearly understood the value of international route authority, particularly Northwest's. They had broached the subject of creating an alliance with NWA the year before, but had been dismissed by Northwest's president, Steve Rothmeier.

As a foreign carrier, KLM was prohibited by US law from controlling a US airline itself. However, as they watched the emerging struggle over Northwest, KLM management determined that if there was to be a change of control, and if they could structure the right relationship, they wanted to back the winner. To that end, they set up meetings with most of the potential bidders identified by the American press.

I received a call the third week in April from Sharyar Aziz of Smith Barney, KLM's US investment bank. Together with Tom Bas, KLM's treasurer, we met in New York. Aziz and Bas explained that KLM desired to invest in one of the possible suitors, and ultimately to develop a future strategic alliance with Northwest Airlines.

I was unenthusiastic. We had not yet been asked to submit a bid by the Northwest board and would not bid unless specifically requested. Also, the Department of Transportation (DOT) did not look with great favor upon the involvement of foreign airlines in the affairs of US domestic carriers; thus, approval of a bid with foreign involvement would be problematic. Besides, I quite simply did not know enough about the airline industry or about Northwest to structure an intelligent agreement, particularly with KLM executives who had the advantage of decades of industry experience.

I suggested that instead of wasting their time and possibly backing the wrong bidder, KLM should wait until the issue of NWA's ownership was resolved. If we were the successful bidder, after we became more familiar with Northwest, the industry and our needs, we would be pleased to talk with them.

KLM disagreed and felt that it was important to be an investor from the outset of the transaction to ensure that a material relationship would develop. I countered that we could not agree out front to limit in any way the future operations or flexibility of NWA. Since we could give KLM no material control (and certainly not veto power) over future decision-making, teaming with us would make no sense. KLM would be investing a huge amount of money as a shareholder with no assurance of ever achieving any benefits as an airline. In the future, they would be totally dependent on our good faith.

I assumed that my candor had effectively ended our discussion. But I had not reckoned on that unique mixture of stubbornness and persistence peculiar to the Dutch, which I would come to recognize with equal parts admiration and exasperation.

A week later, Kathy and I were visiting the Elliotts in France when I received another call from KLM. Could we meet again to continue our discussion of KLM's investment in Wings? I was stunned. KLM sent a small plane to take us to Amsterdam. They provided Kathy a guided tour of the city while I was taken directly to KLM's corporate headquarters. I was ushered into a conference room where a dozen of KLM's top managers, including its chairman, Jan de Soet, and president, Pieter Bouw, were seated across a large table. They wanted to hear firsthand my philosophy of management and our strategy for Northwest Airlines.

Unencumbered by modesty, I proceeded to lay out our guiding principles and our plans. Yet as I sat there, alone on my side of the table, and gazed upon the faces of men who collectively, by my reckoning, had over two hundred and fifty years of airline experience, I felt not only presumptuous, but more than a little ridiculous.

Later that evening Pieter Bouw and his wife, Janni, hosted us at their home for dinner with three other top KLM executives and their wives. Kathy, as usual, was captivating. At the end of the evening, Pieter Bouw turned to me and said, "If Kathy Checchi married you, so will we." And that was it. Within two weeks KLM had committed $400 million toward our acquisition of Northwest Airlines.

We had no contractual commitments beyond our relationship as shareholders and only a general memorandum outlining the possible areas for future collaboration on the operating side. The rest was left to faith. Kathy had clinched our seventh and final partner.

On April 25, unable to prevent the Davis tender offer, the NWA board relented and announced that it would establish a bidding process and make confidential information available to all qualified entities interested in acquiring the airline. NWA would be auctioned to the highest bidder. That same day, the *New York Post* confirmed that KKR, the country's premier leveraged-buyout firm, was among the dozen potential bidders.

Marvin Davis dropped his tender offer and agreed to abide by the rules of the bidding process established by NWA. On May 4, the *Wall Street Journal* reported that at long last Wings Partners, aided by Bankers Trust Corporation, had formally agreed to submit an offer to purchase Northwest Airlines.

Over the ensuing weeks, many groups presented themselves to examine the Northwest books. In addition to our group, KKR, and Davis, interest was expressed by the leveraged-buyout firms of Kelso & Company, Forstmann Little, and MEI Diversified, a company controlled by Minneapolis investor Carl Pohlad. On May 6, Guy Cook, president of IAM Air Transport District 43, announced that his union was exploring a buyout in which it would team up with an as-yet-undetermined "patient investor." Based on my personal experience with investors, he would have better luck finding a unicorn.

On May 15, it was our turn to access Northwest's management and records to perform due diligence, the process by which a buyer evaluates a potential acquisition. We soon found that to accomplish our due

diligence and assemble the mountain of documentation needed to structure and finance the acquisition of Northwest Airlines required a small
army.

What started out as a cottage industry involving Gary Wilson and
myself had expanded dramatically. Each of the five other partners con-
tributed to the effort. Bankers Trust deployed a large group to inventory all of the financial obligations of NWA. This included aircraft and
facilities leases and every lien on every piece of property. Richard Blum
deployed two analysts from his investment fund to aid in evaluating
NWA's business operations. Elders added three of its merchant bankers,
and KLM sent over a contingent of operating and strategic management
specialists to help analyze NWA's future prospects. Added to this were
key personnel from my own growing merchant bank: Alex Goodwin, an
entrepreneur and specialist in executive search; Linda Levinson, a former
McKinsey & Company partner and travel expert; James Cronin, former
chief executive officer of Tiger International, a major air freight company;
Len Busse, former senior vice president of Continental Bank, an experienced credit officer; and Tom McLain, former partner of Manatt, Phelps
& Phillips LLP, an international lawyer with extensive Asian experience.
We added personnel from a host of outside service providers—the law
firm of Simpson Thacher & Bartlett; advisors Wasserstein Perella & Co.;
the accounting firm of Deloitte, Haskins & Sells; Simat Helliesen and
Eichner, an airline consulting firm; Martin Shugrue, an independent consultant who later became trustee of Eastern Airlines; and the Washington
regulatory law firm of Verner, Liipfert, Bernhard, McPherson and Hand.
We were, to borrow Randall Smith's word, "serious."

We had assembled what many considered one of the most credentialed teams and performed one of the most professional due-diligence
efforts of any significant transaction of the 1980s. Many days, I have
looked back with wonder at all this assembled excellence and leafed
through the impressive documentation that we produced. Paraphrasing
Churchill, never had so many produced so much that went so wrong.
With all that brilliant talent, no one had accounted for the future actions
of a man named Saddam Hussein.

The pressure during this period was unrelenting. I was coordinating the activities of scores of people and trying to reconcile the competing interests of at least a dozen entities. Meanwhile, the press was reporting a steady drumbeat of rumors in an effort to handicap the competing bidders. Adding to the drama, the DOT asserted in a letter its own intent to scrutinize carefully the managerial competence and financial capability of any proposed NWA owner and to use its broad authority to overturn any agreement that it deemed "not in the public interest."

Meanwhile we were slowly emerging as the local favorite. Rothmeier had been comparatively complimentary. Although we were newcomers, the national press had been extraordinarily positive, focusing on our corporate track records. I judged that labor would be critical to success, so with the company's permission, I met with each of NWA's unions. In a key statement, Guy Cook of the IAM announced on May 20 that he might look favorably on a bid from us, based not only on our meeting but some of our prior work with the IAM (Gary and I had received union endorsement years earlier when the US government was considering a sale of Conrail). Cook said, "I think we could find ways to assist someone who made a commitment to operating this airline, rather than liquidating its assets." He went on to add a stern warning for all potential bidders: "I certainly know we can make trouble for someone who would jeopardize our members' jobs."

On May 30, 1989, in accordance with the terms established by the Northwest board, we submitted our bid.

In submitting our bid, consistent with the objectives that we had established nearly seven months earlier, we had assembled a group of strategic investors with extensive individual and institutional business experience and significant additional financial resources that could be deployed on behalf of NWA if the need arose. Further, we had structured one of the most conservative financing packages of any leveraged transaction completed that decade.

We invested $700 million of equity, an enormous amount by 1980s standards. This was more equity than had been employed in any buyout during the previous ten years, with the exception of the $1 billion of equity invested by KKR in acquiring R.J. Reynolds (RJR). However, the total purchase price of RJR was over six times as large as that of NWA, making the RJR equity far smaller, in percentage terms.

In structuring the acquisition debt, we recognized that NWA was unique in a highly leveraged industry. It was virtually debt-free. We proceeded to raise only that amount of debt that would bring NWA's leverage to the levels maintained by its major competitors. We used no high-yield or "junk bond" financing, but obtained a single, comparatively simple and straightforward commercial bank term loan. In this respect, our financing was uniquely conservative, certainly when compared with the other bids received by NWA.

The call sheet containing the names and phone numbers of all the persons involved in the preparation of our bid numbered an even seventy people. We were all drained by the effort to meet the May 30 deadline. At the end, we felt like marathoners. We had been running so long that when we finally stopped, we were disoriented. In our minds, we had won by completing the race, and as we congratulated each other, the outcome and final standings hardly mattered.

This feeling of exhilaration, unspoiled by any sense of competition, lasted approximately twenty-four hours. We quickly reverted to form, scouring the newspapers and grasping at every rumor, however specious, in a vain attempt to determine what the other bidders had proposed and how the board members were disposed. The deliberations of the board, however, were impenetrable. My hat was off to them. NWA was playing its hand masterfully.

On June 5, the NWA board announced that there was no clear winner. The board asked all bidders to resubmit bids by June 16 and to address directly the concerns expressed in a recent letter from the US Transportation Secretary, Sam Skinner. These included the effects of the added debt burden on NWA and the managerial competence and financial capability of the bidders.

The reaction of our group was anger. We doubted that any bidder had remotely made as complete and fully financed a proposal as we (our subsequent review of the bid proposals would later confirm this). We had triggered very substantial bank commitment fees in submitting a fully financed bid. The costs for our lawyers and the technical experts employed in our submission were also significant. There was substantial support among our group to drop out of the bidding process altogether and sell our shares to the winner, at a significant profit.

After much discussion, however, the sentiments that had driven us to express interest in NWA in the first place prevailed. We wanted to run and grow the company and tackle the challenge of building the world's first global airline, and we believed in our vision of how to do it. We resubmitted a bid.

The phone in my Los Angeles home rang at eight o'clock Saturday morning, June 17, 1989. It was Bob Friedman: "They want to meet us in New York tomorrow morning." "You must be kidding," I complained. "It's Father's Day."

After ten months, countless meetings and presentations, five or six feet of legal documents, thousands of miles shuttling around three continents, numerous sprints up blind alleys, and a torrent of often conflicting emotions, the long and tortuous quest to acquire control of the world's fourth-largest airline was going to come down to a single meeting.

Northwest did not fly nonstop from Los Angeles to New York City. Kathy and I rushed to catch the last American Airlines flight to New York. As the plane headed east, with Kathy buckled in next to me for moral support, I wondered how this next chapter would unfold.

On Sunday, June 18, at ten a.m., I arrived at the law offices of Fried, Frank, Harris, Shriver, & Jacobson in New York City. There I met NWA's chief outside counsel, Steve Fraidin, a Fried Frank partner, and Jim Maher, a partner with First Boston, NWA's investment bank. Bob Friedman, my attorney, had already arrived, as well as Sharyar Aziz, KLM's investment banker. Fred Malek joined us later in the day. After coffee and small talk centered around family (after all, it was Father's Day), we got down to business.

Apparently we had been the high bidder and our financing package was viewed quite favorably, as was the composition of the team that we had assembled. We then turned to the merger agreement itself. This document would set the terms and conditions for closing the transaction, as well as the penalties for failure to achieve certain conditions precedent to closing. Given the reams of documentation that we had already produced and the full price that we had agreed to pay ($121 per share), this might seem a relatively straightforward exercise. But, as Ross Perot often observed, "The devil is in the details."

We negotiated for more than twelve hours. Important to us were the representations and warranties of the company. What if they neglected to tell us a material fact or failed to disclose exposure to a pending liability? How could we be protected? From the company's standpoint, what if we failed to obtain DOT approval or Congress passed new legislation blocking us from taking control? What if Bankers Trust was unable to syndicate the loan? What penalty would we pay? Important to both of us, what if the pilots made good their threat to strike? Who would make decisions for NWA during the interim period between signing the merger document and closing? What commitments could be made? If the deal closed, we would be liable for actions taken on behalf of NWA. If the deal failed to close, NWA's existing shareholders would bear responsibility.

These were difficult issues, and they were not win-win. We were discussing the consequences of failure and the responsibility for its costs. This was not an academic exercise; the risks were great. Except under conditions of extreme economic duress, not only had no one ever taken an airline private (out of the realm of public ownership), no one had ever acquired an airline as large as NWA. There were powerful forces in Congress and at the DOT who were predisposed to resist change, in particular change that offered no political benefits. The NWA unions had already voiced strong opposition to any buyout. Irrespective of their feelings about the company's present management, union leaders, like other political leaders, had nothing to gain from a change in control of NWA. They had no direct experience with us. To them we would always be, at best, just another group of capitalists.

Also, the unions deplored debt. They had learned through bitter experience that they had little power over lenders. If debt covenants (the conditions imposed by lenders) were violated and debt holders exercised their legal rights to force a company into bankruptcy proceeding, no amount of labor action could prevent it. In bankruptcy, unions, like other constituents, lost significant rights. Union contracts could be voided and lower wage rates and more liberal work rules could be imposed by the courts. Small wonder that union leaders universally opposed leveraged acquisitions.

In addition to the terms and conditions relating to closing, NWA's negotiators insisted on incorporating other provisions into the merger agreement. They wanted to provide payments to NWA's top management in the event that their employment was terminated after the acquisition. These agreements, known as "golden parachutes," were not uncommon in merger agreements. However, they usually provided protection to management only in the event of arbitrary dismissal or significant diminishment of responsibility. The provisions proposed by NWA were extraordinarily liberal. They basically provided that NWA's top managers could choose to terminate employment themselves and still collect payments.

We could have refused these terms. The NWA board would scarcely terminate our discussions over the issue of protecting managers who arbitrarily quit their jobs. But the total potential dollar exposure of the payments was not large. We had been given no reason to believe that management would not want to continue in place, since we intended to build the business, not liquidate it, and we had no intention of managing the business ourselves. We also wanted to show confidence, support, and willingness to work with existing NWA management, albeit with a stated shift of strategic direction. We accepted the NWA proposal, but soon came to regret this gesture of accommodation.

Negotiation of the merger agreement continued until approximately two the following morning. The NWA board signaled its approval of the terms, and I signed the agreement on behalf of Wings Holdings Incorporated. I was elated. Bob Friedman teared up as he congratulated me. We had known each other nearly fifteen years, and he knew full well the significance of this moment for me.

I returned to the Hotel Plaza Athenee about an hour later. Kathy, whom I had called to report every two hours during the long day, was still waiting up to hear the final results. "The Eagle has landed," I announced as I entered the room.

We talked until almost sunrise about the last nine months, the people we had met, the places we had gone, the things we had done, the emotions we had felt. I reached back further into the past as I tried to comprehend the totality of the events that had driven me to this place, so far from where I had begun.

Drained by the experiences of this long day, I turned to shut off the light beside our bed. It was five thirty in the morning. As I lay in the sudden darkness, I felt a rush of fear mixed with exhilaration: "My God, I'm responsible for 40,000 people."

ELEVEN
The End of the Beginning

Now this is not the end. It is not even the beginning of the end.
But it is, perhaps, the end of the beginning.

Winston Churchill

I GREETED THE SEVEN-A.M. wake-up call with all the enthusiasm of a sharp
stick in the eye. The Eagle had crashed. I was nearly out on my feet as
I fumbled to answer the bell for the second round.

We had not exactly bought an airline. We had, at best, rented one.
Confirming the truth of our situation, the NWA merger agreement provided an entire year, until June 30, 1990, to complete the transaction.
There was also so little confidence that we could succeed in harnessing
the combined forces of labor, government, and the financial community
that the contracts contained no penalties if we failed to close.

My morning started ominously in a photography studio on the east
side of Manhattan. When, midway through Sunday afternoon, it had
appeared that we would negotiate a merger agreement, Bob Friedman
had asked who would handle our publicity. I assumed that we would
continue as before. "No one," I said.

Bob explained, quite patiently in retrospect, that we were proposing
to acquire a highly regulated major American corporation employing a

90-percent unionized work force and providing vital service to approximately 200 American cities—not a hotel in Dubuque. We would need a professional financial public relations firm to manage media inquiries as we proceeded to convince labor and government at multiple levels, as well as the broad international financial community, that NWA would be in safe hands. David Duffy of the public relations firm of Adams & Rinehart joined us that afternoon. Now we were seventy-one.

While Duffy directed a press photo shoot, I talked my way through approximately twenty telephone interviews with representatives of the national press and local press from cities with significant NWA operations. These proceeded reasonably well until Ron Grover of *Business Week* asked if I was concerned about our ability to raise the remaining funding.

Raising money seemed to me the least of our problems, and having known Ron from my Disney days, I retorted, "Ron, what do you think this is, amateur night at the Roxie?" Ron had his quote and he had gotten it fair and square. During the weeks following its appearance in *Business Week*, the specter of failure would constantly haunt me, in the form of one of my newly minted photos captioned "Amateur Night at the Roxie." Thankfully, it never happened, but I learned my lesson. I would not make this mistake again. Years later, when the quote "Debt is your friend" was repeatedly and mistakenly attributed to me, I lived with the irony of being connected with something that I *didn't* say.

Having survived my somewhat shaky start with the press, I left David to clean up the broken glass. He did an extraordinary job over the ensuing weeks, persuading a congenitally skeptical press corps that we were basically what we said we were: a group of responsible corporate executives and institutions intent on building and growing a company, not liquidating it.

Analyzing our situation, I concluded that the acquisition of NWA could not be accomplished in a year. We would have to move much faster or be overwhelmed by the forces of inertia. Contradicting the conventional wisdom, I resolved to close the acquisition by September 1, in just ten weeks.

Establishing positive relations with NWA's existing management would be important. I therefore resolved that my first official act as an "owner-elect" of Northwest Airlines should be to visit management. Since Kathy had made such a favorable impression dining with a Dutchman, I decided to try her on the German Steve Rothmeier. We boarded a Twin Cities–bound Northwest flight at LaGuardia Airport shortly after five p.m.

When we emerged from the walkway into Minneapolis–Saint Paul International Airport, we were greeted by an explosion of light. Through the blinding glare I could make out a half-dozen television cameras and a crush of people with microphones, still cameras, and recording devices. I had previously conducted my professional and personal life in virtual anonymity. Bob Friedman was right. This was definitely not a hotel in Dubuque.

As we pushed through the gathering of reporters and equipment, mindful of my morning's performance with Ron Grover, I responded to the shouted questions with my best Ronald Reagan impersonation. Smiling broadly, my right hand cupped to my right ear, my other arm alternately around Kathy and waving, I continued walking briskly through the terminal.

We proceeded to the Registry Hotel, where we encountered yet another gauntlet of reporters. This time I paused to murmur a few disjointed platitudes about NWA and the Twin Cities. Mindful that I was in the hometown of the legendary Hubert Humphrey, I felt like his character in the old Vaughn Meader comedy album burbling, "I'm pleased as punch to be here."

The scene changed as we entered the dining room. There, seated at a table dwarfed by his large frame, was Steve Rothmeier, Northwest's chairman and chief executive officer. He rose to greet Kathy and me as we approached. Rothmeier stood over six feet with the heavy, muscled body of a middle-aged linebacker. He was bald, with eyes distorted by the thick wire-rimmed glasses he wore. He looked much older than his forty-three years.

Early newspaper accounts had heralded our deal as a great victory for Rothmeier, who seemed, according to the *St. Paul Pioneer Press*, "to have maneuvered a hostile takeover fight into the best possible outcome for management." During the morning's interviews, I had reiterated that we wanted Rothmeier and his team to stay, that we intended to maintain corporate headquarters in the Twin Cities, and that we would continue the company's $4-billion fleet expansion program.

Steve Rothmeier, the oldest of three sons, was a native Minnesotan born in Mankato, a town south of the Twin Cities. According to published reports, his grandfather arrived in Minnesota from Germany, bringing with him an immigrant's strong work ethic and the equally strong Catholic religious beliefs that Steve would embrace. He had been a fine high-school football player who made the University of Notre Dame squad as a walk-on. A career-ending injury in his sophomore year led him to redirect his energies to his studies. Called "Sparty" by his classmates for his Spartan regimen, Rothmeier left school at the age of twenty in order to run the family propane business following his father's death in an automobile accident. After negotiating the sale of the family business, he returned to Notre Dame and graduated, earned a Bronze Star while serving in Vietnam, and acquired an MBA from the University of Chicago.

He had joined NWA in April 1973 as a financial analyst recruited by Don Nyrop, the company's legendary and irascible chairman. By 1982 he was elected president and chief operating officer by the board under Joe Lapensky, Nyrop's successor. He became chairman in 1986. In 1989, at the age of forty-three, he was still the youngest chief executive officer of a major airline.

USA Today said Rothmeier "isn't exactly the life of the party. He expects his officers to work two Saturdays a month if necessary. . . . With his German background, he's very pragmatic. He's not a party boy. He lives near headquarters in a castle-style mansion. He never married." The *Star Tribune* added: "Rothmeier is a reserved man, not easy to know and, to an outsider, appears cool and aloof. His conservative management style has been criticized; labor leaders consider him impersonal. 'He's a number cruncher, and a people cruncher,' Teamsters representative William Genoese said."

Rothmeier's tenure as chairman had been, according to the *Star Tribune*, "marked by tumult, post-merger complications after the acquisition of Republic Airlines . . . and labor troubles [that] repeatedly raised the specter of strike." The merger had been a defining moment for Rothmeier and NWA. According to the *Detroit Free Press*, "Few people understood how tricky it would be to blend the airlines' dissimilar fleets, schedules, work forces, and most important, styles. . . . Republic employees were used to a management that wasn't so autocratic, that was more people-oriented. What followed was a cascade of chaos."

Rothmeier was indeed reserved. We had no preexisting relationship. I had met him only briefly at the start of our due diligence. At dinner that evening, we made small talk about the events of the past few weeks and the recent performance of NWA, but our conversation was notably impersonal. I tend to connect relatively easily with people, and Kathy is particularly engaging, but we both noted how difficult it had been to carry on the evening's conversation. Rothmeier was not disagreeable. He actually had a nice smile. He was neither cold nor hostile; neither did he seem anxious or uncomfortable. He was like a black hole, emitting no light. During our final meeting a few weeks later, he said to me, "I don't want anyone to know me." He had nothing to fear. To this day, I don't have a clue as to what motivates this very private man.

The next morning, NWA sent a limousine to take me to the headquarters building. As I left the hotel, maybe out of some sixth sense or possibly from residual anxiety over my crack to *Business Week*, I hesitated and waved off the limousine and opted instead for the taxi parked behind it. Consequently, when I arrived at NWA corporate headquarters, another gauntlet of television cameras captured an unexpectedly young man (I had just turned forty-one) emerging from an old taxi, carrying his own garment bag, and bantering good-naturedly with the driver. Images such as this one, informal interviews that I gave, and secondhand commentary from employees, government officials, and community leaders whom I met combined to give an impression (hopefully true) that I was a regular guy who didn't take himself too seriously.

These positive impressions, drawn more sharply because of their apparent contrast with Rothmeier, were both a blessing and a curse. I learned that the next worst thing to bad press is good press. The first hint came a few days later in the *Star Tribune*. Columnist Dick Youngblood wrote, "Folks around here have started sounding like they might canonize Checchi. . . . The consensus seems to be that Checchi is a so-called white knight, a savior who somehow has snatched the airline from the clutches of greedy sharpies bent on dismembering it. One TV anchor burbled that the man is 'too good to be true.' Has everyone lost their senses . . . ? White knights, my Aunt Fannie; white sharks would be more accurate." Fortunately, Youngblood was a lone voice during these early heady weeks.

Unsurprisingly, at NWA headquarters I found the senior management team no more forthcoming than Rothmeier. Unlike the team at Marriott and Disney, these were rigid people, resistant to change, and suspicious of outsiders and each other. The atmosphere seemed a throwback to the 1950s: hierarchical, militaristic, and closed. It was not a fun place.

Although management had much to gain personally from the acquisition, the same could not be said for labor. Organized labor is among the country's more reactionary institutions. Labor abhors change, and nowhere is change resisted more, it seems, than in the transportation industry. This resistance is built into the very structure of the collective bargaining process. Airline labor law is governed by the National Railway Labor Act. Designed to establish a series of trip wires to mitigate against frivolous or precipitous work stoppages of rail passenger and freight service, the National Railway Labor Act virtually assures that contract resolution pursued under its authority will proceed at a glacial pace. Under the terms of the act, labor contracts do not expire; they merely become amendable.

Once a contract reaches the end of its term, labor and management proceed through a series of elaborate steps until the government permits them, in essence, to agree to disagree. An amalgamation of rules constituting "negotiating in good faith" creates a labyrinth through which the participants must pass. Like a great game of Chutes and Ladders, the participants continue until they are tripped up by some procedural error, at which time they are sent back to the beginning. When the parties at last reach a certain level, they earn the help of the federal government in the form of a mediator assigned by the National Labor Mediation Board. This mediator has no authority to impose a binding settlement, but the parties continue to be dependent on the mediation board, since only after satisfying the board and participating in yet another round of procedures may they eventually gain release from mediation.

In releasing the parties from mediation, the board allows the parties to disagree (to a point) and declares an impasse. This triggers a thirty-day "cooling-off" period, during which the parties are encouraged to bargain in earnest. At the end of the thirty-day cooling-off period, if no agreement is reached and assuming that there are no further technical procedural infractions, management is finally free to implement its last offer and labor is free to strike. What a way to run a railroad!

NWA and its pilots had been proceeding according to these rules for three years, since July 1986, and had yet to be released to start a cooling-off period.

The true genius of Northwest labor relations, however, was that they were so acrimonious that somehow the parties were able to negotiate this tortuous labyrinth to make Northwest the most strike-prone airline in America: five strikes in a dozen years (1970, 1972, 1975, 1978, and 1982). Northwest labor relations would deteriorate further in the late 1980s. The 1986 merger of Northwest with Republic Airlines caused employees from these two radically different cultures to be shuffled together like playing cards. Individual work assignments and, equally important, the locations of those work assignments, previously based on the seniority of two separate work forces, were reassigned based on a single combined seniority list. This was a wrenching experience for the employees of both companies, but nowhere was the disruption greater or the rancor deeper than among the pilots.

Divided into Red Book (old Northwest pilots who flew according to a contract bound in red) and Green Book (old Republic pilots who similarly were governed by a contract bound in green), the two pilot groups at NWA had yet to reach agreement on a new combined contract (later to be bound in gray). Forced to fly in the same cockpit, pilots from these two separate groups often did not converse, save for the minimum required to operate an aircraft safely. The two pilot groups were pitted against each other in a three-way negotiation that included an unsympathetic NWA management bent on dividing and conquering them. It was an extraordinary spectacle. I thought of a potential movie: *Godzilla Meets the Hatfields and the McCoys!*

It was into this three-ringed circus that I ventured on Tuesday afternoon to meet with representatives from the combined Red Book and Green Book Master Executive Council (MEC), the elected local governing body of the Air Line Pilots Association (ALPA), the powerful union representing the 5,100 pilots of Northwest Airlines. None of the six Northwest unions ostensibly had anything to gain from the buyout. Three of the largest unions (ALPA, the IAM, and the Teamsters, who represented the flight attendants) had the ability to stop the closing. Because banks would not deliberately expose themselves to labor strife, these unions could frustrate our efforts to obtain our financing. Guy Cook of the IAM had publicly indicated some preliminary interest in our group, and the Teamsters had expressed optimism that the labor-relations environment might improve with the removal of Rothmeier. The pilots, however, had been most reticent, and they were a significant problem. They had been negotiating a contract with NWA for three years and could soon seek release from the mediation board and call for a strike. By meeting with them first, I signaled my appreciation of their position.

I began the meeting by stating that we would not attempt to close the acquisition of NWA if there was active opposition by the pilots. We were managers who wished to grow a business, not fight with employees. I described our background. None of us had any appreciable experience with organized labor. We were, therefore, not veterans of the historic labor-management struggle. Where we had come from, we were all considered employees. Distinctions between labor and management, per se, did not exist. They looked at me like I had landed from another planet, but at least they were listening.

I acknowledged the huge stake that pilots have in the future of

Northwest and their legitimate interests in understanding our plans for the future. I offered to open our books to the MEC and their financial advisor and to make myself and our staff available to answer their most minute questions. Over the next several weeks, the MEC and their advisors participated in a series of detailed presentations. They questioned every number, traced every forecasted airplane delivery, and generally immersed themselves in every detail of every line item in our plan. Reflecting their training and background, their interest in minutia was insatiable.

In short order, all the pilots had the details of our deal. Later, when I was invited up to a cockpit by a 757 captain, he said that I had done a pretty good job putting the Northwest deal together, but . . . He proceeded to unfold a large spreadsheet like a map across the plane's windshield and explain to me how *he* would have done it. During the ensuing two years, nearly every trip to the cockpit would be the same. The pilots would take the opportunity to tell me how to run the business in great detail: what routes we should change, how we should price, what we were doing wrong with flight operations, the equipment that we should buy, etc. I resisted the urge and never once told a pilot how to fly a plane, but the apparent irony was lost on them.

Pilots are control freaks. They thrive on routine, and that's what keeps passengers and equipment safe. Nothing in their world is left to chance. Before they take off, not only do they know where they're going, but exactly how they'll get there, at what altitude and speed, how many checkpoints they will refer to along the way, the arrival time practically to the minute, the weight of the passengers and the cargo, and the amount of fuel that they will burn. They have a predetermined secondary city, and even a third one, in the event of adverse weather conditions or ground problems. They proceed down a long mechanical and electrical checklist, and even today must complete a visual external inspection of the aircraft before every departure. The backup systems on a modern commercial aircraft have backups and the pilots check all of these, too.

Pilots have to be well-trained and disciplined, because if they make a mistake, it can be fatal. A good pilot needs confidence, and it shows, sometimes inducing a certain macho grandiosity. There is a story, often told by flight attendants, of the young boy who says, "When I grow up, I want to be a pilot." His mother turns to him and says, "Son, you can't have it both ways." Yet there is also another saying: "There are old pilots and bold pilots, but there are no old, bold pilots." A good pilot is by nature a blend of self-confidence and caution. Understandably, a pilots union is a difficult organization to manage. As one union official said of the NWA pilots union, "We have 5,100 chiefs and no Indians."

The first labor dispute in aviation history was initiated by a pilot. In 1919, an airmail pilot named Leon Smith, nicknamed "Bonehead" because he once walked into a whirling propeller and survived, refused to fly. The reason was fog. When he was fired, the other pilots struck in support, and four days later management relented and reinstated Bonehead. Since early aviation was dangerous, pilots became more assertive about issues of safety. Consequently, the Air Line Pilots Association (ALPA) was formed in the early 1930s.

Contract negotiations for the pilots of an airline like NWA are conducted by the local Master Executive Council (MEC). At NWA, the MEC is composed of approximately two dozen pilots, each elected by pilot constituents grouped by aircraft type, position, and geographic base (e.g., 747 captains based in Los Angeles). Because the individual MEC members are highly independent and strongly opinionated, their decision-making is byzantine. Like the College of Cardinals, the MEC members meet in private and proceed in their own way at their own pace. Outsiders can only wait, eyes trained on the chimney, searching for traces of smoke to indicate if a decision has been made. We waited expectantly for five weeks to see if our acquisition could proceed. When it finally appeared, the smoke was first green, followed by red.

As reported in the July 19 *Pioneer Press*, "Checchi's bid received a curious boost from 2,200 Northwest pilots who used to work for Republic." The following day, the *Wall Street Journal* reported, "A second group of pilots said it will support Checchi. A group representing about 2,800 of Northwest's 5,000 pilots said Checchi's business plan appears viable." Although they had reached their decisions separately,

Green and Red had at least agreed on something. This was an important start for the healing process at NWA.

NWA's flight dispatchers were represented by the Transport Workers Union. The dispatchers are a small group, but their function is critical to an airline. It is the dispatchers who calculate how much fuel an airplane must carry based on aircraft type, distance, wind speed, and weight. Weight is affected by the number of people boarded, their baggage, and additional cargo carried. While airlines do not actually weigh people, they work from estimated national averages—except for flights in Wisconsin, Iowa, and Minnesota, known as the "fat belt," where several pounds are added to the estimates.

The amount of fuel carried is sufficient to fly to the primary destination plus a second alternative airport plus a 15 percent "captain's minimum" for reserve. Carrying too much fuel has its cost, which is the cost of burning additional fuel to transport the excess. Yet airlines frequently carry surplus fuel on selected flights based on the calculated costs of refueling in different locations. For example, a plane scheduled to fly to Nevada and then on to Los Angeles might take on extra fuel in Nevada because fuel is more expensive in Los Angeles. Dispatchers make these types of calculations.

Once a Northwest flight is airborne, the dispatchers continue to track its progress from a command center at the Minneapolis–Saint Paul International Airport. Working from computer screens, much like air traffic controllers, they communicate continuously with Northwest flights, advising of changing weather conditions or airport congestion, perhaps changing speed, altitude, or routing to adjust for changes that have occurred either in the air or on the ground. Safety is paramount, but there are considerations of passenger convenience and comfort (on-time performance, smoothness of flight) and cost (fuel-burn) that also affect these decisions.

The dispatchers also handle irregularities. For an airline the size of Northwest, there are in-flight medical emergencies about three times per week on average (such as heart attack, coma, choking, and baby delivery). There are mechanical failures, which may dictate rerouting the aircraft or may be corrected midair in consultation with ground personnel. There are also myriad other human conditions, such as passenger drunkenness or belligerence, threats or hijacking.

Managing 1,500 flights per day carrying over 150,000 people and tons of cargo to nearly 300 airports worldwide in an atmosphere of ever-changing weather conditions, air-traffic congestion, gate changes, medical emergencies, and a range of passenger behavioral problems, the Northwest dispatchers were too busy to worry about our acquisition of the airline. Their leaders expressed amazement that anyone would invest in such an uncertain business, wished us luck, and resumed watching their screens.

The meteorologists, like the dispatchers, have their own small union. They are the lynchpin of the scheduling process. Hundreds of thousands of dollars can rest on a weather prediction, particularly if that prediction means canceling flights. Wind costs money and snow costs money (I soon learned that everything costs money in this business). Given the hub system of interconnecting flights through a series of concentrated locations in the United States, high winds or snow in Boston can affect the travel plans of a lawyer in Minneapolis heading west, a tourist in Los Angeles, or a heart patient in Seattle traveling to the Mayo Clinic in Rochester. Depending on the actual or expected severity of the weather, an entire airline system may have to be rescheduled. The meteorologists work closely with the dispatchers, and their attitudes toward us were similar. They, too, were too busy to notice us.

The IAM is one of the most militant trade unions in the United States. While ALPA has great power, given its members' ability to ground a fleet, pilots, with their advanced degrees and burgeoning stock portfolios, are hardly traditional trade unionists. Many pursue dual professions, as their flying hours are limited by the Federal Aviation Administration (FAA). If pilots embody the capitalist ideal and big business, then the IAM defines the term "big labor."

Led by the legendary Bill Winpisinger for twelve years until his retirement in 1989, the IAM is a muscular union comprised principally of machinists and mechanics in aircraft, automotive, and railroad manufacturing and maintenance. These are mostly tough, hard-hitting, straightforward, no-nonsense blue-collar types who have flown the flags of most of labor's principle battles since the 1930s. From time to time, they were a tremendous source of unexpected malapropisms at critical moments; one high official sternly warning me during a contentious negotiation, "Just remember, the penguin swings both ways!"

At Northwest, in the bitter aftermath of the Republic merger, the IAM extended its representation beyond its more traditional boundaries. Not only did the IAM represent the mechanics, machinists, and ramp personnel at NWA, but also the reservations agents, the customer-service agents, the luggage handlers, and even most of the clerical staff. All told, the IAM represented almost half of Northwest's 40,000 employees. Given the scope of its representation, the IAM could, like the pilots, shut down the airline.

The local head of the IAM was Guy Cook. Normally soft-spoken, almost professorial, he could raise his voice to a window-rattling shout midsentence when angered. He had earned a reputation for toughness and extraordinary independence not only with NWA management, who considered him the devil incarnate, but also within his own union, where he operated with extraordinary autonomy. This was particularly remarkable given his background as a luggage handler in a union dominated by its "elite" skilled mechanics.

Although a dyed-in-the-wool trade unionist, Cook came to realize earlier than most labor leaders that the old paradigm of labor-management conflict no longer worked. Deregulation of the airline industry in 1978 had destroyed the employees' safety net. Airlines could now fail and, as they did with growing regularity, working people got hurt.

A unionized airline employee derives his status and compensation from seniority. Seniority is the Holy Grail, but it cannot be transported; it is company-specific. The twenty-five-year airline captain who lost his $175,000-per-year job with the collapse of Eastern Airlines forfeited his seniority. If he was lucky enough to be hired by another airline, Northwest, for example, he started at the bottom of the NWA seniority list as a second officer, behind the other 5,100 Northwest pilots, and earned approximately $25,000. The same is true for all other trades. If you lose your position at one airline, you start over in another—if you can get a job.

Guy Cook could see what was happening as one carrier after another failed. He could also understand, because he had lived through it, how wrenching an airline merger could be even if it did save jobs, particularly when labor and management were at odds. He understood that to survive over the next decade, labor and management would have to overcome their deep, decades-old distrust and try to find some common ground to build a new working relationship. It would not be easy. Labor-management relations in the industry were highly adversarial. At Northwest, the mutual hatred was palpable. Elected union leaders were not allowed on the grounds of the company's corporate headquarters. In union halls, Rothmeier and his managers were hanged in effigy. Comparisons with Hitler and his storm troopers were not uncommon.

Perhaps because several of Cook's legal and business advisors knew me previously, or because I had earned my wealth personally and had participated in building companies, not dismantling them, or maybe because I was comparatively young and had no experience with the industry's struggles—for whatever reasons, Guy Cook decided to take a chance with us. The IAM would not block our closing, but Cook made it clear they would hold us to the principles that we espoused.

After meeting with the pilot MEC and Guy Cook, I flew to Washington, DC to meet with the Teamsters. If the IAM under Guy Cook pursued a comparatively conciliatory approach to the acquisition of Northwest, Bill Genoese of the IBT would present, at least initially, a different face of organized labor. Representing Northwest's nearly 10,000 flight attendants, the leaders of the rough-and-tumble Teamsters (the union once headed by the notorious Jimmy Hoffa) stood in contrast with the flight attendants whom they represented.

Years later, while I was engaged in a difficult negotiation, one other malapropism-prone union official punctuated an impassioned description of the role of the modern-day flight attendant. "These people have to do everything. Why, if someone is choking, they even have to be able to do that hymen maneuver!"

The "hymen maneuver" excepted, the modern-day flight attendant does have a great deal of responsibility. Like many jobs in the airline industry, the flight attendant's has evolved over time.

Although airlines were desperate in their early days to attract passengers, it never occurred to them to hire flight attendants, certainly not women. In 1930 Steve Simpson, the manager of Boeing's San Francisco office, proposed to hire stewards—Filipino men who could move around easily in the cramped cabins, much like stewards on US Navy ships. Then Ellen Church, a San Francisco nurse and flying enthusiast, walked into his office. Church proposed that Boeing hire women. Simpson shot off a memorandum to headquarters explaining "his" idea:

"It strikes me that there would be great psychological punch to have young women stewardesses or couriers. . . . I have in mind a couple of graduate nurses. Imagine the psychology of having young women as regular members of the crew. Imagine the national publicity. . . . Also, imagine the value they would be to us, not only in the neater and nicer method of serving food but looking out for the passengers' welfare."

What went unsaid or, more precisely, unwritten was that attractive flight attendants would give passengers something better to look at than baggage. Ellen Church became the first chief "stewardess." She and the seven other nurse–flight attendants that Boeing hired had to be under twenty-five years old, weigh less than 115 pounds, and stand under sixty-four inches tall. They wore uniforms of green twill and were considered expendable. If no seats were available on a flight, attendants sat on mail sacks. If the plane weighed too much to climb over the mountains, pilots landed, put off a flight attendant or two, and took off again. One important responsibility was to make sure that passengers on their way to the lavatory didn't accidentally open the exit door instead.

But passengers who were fearful of flying were comforted by the presence of these trained nurses. As flying became safer and more commonplace, the nursing degree requirement was dropped. Safety was something airline executives did not want to advertise. Comfort and service instead were stressed. Stewardesses became symbols of that service. They wore white gloves and they were trained to pamper passengers. Some airlines capitalized on their stewardesses by promoting them as available young women looking for husbands. This emphasis on sex appeal and availability led to further exploitation as passengers began to regard stewardesses as sexy servants. Stewardesses became victims of sexual harassment and outright insult. With passage of the 1964 Civil Rights Act and with the emergence of the women's movement, flight attendants obtained greater rights and more respect.

Today's flight attendant at Northwest Airlines must be over the age of twenty, a high-school graduate, and at least sixty-two inches tall (a threshold considered important for safety). They are no longer required to be single or to quit if they are pregnant or have children. They need not be female or have classic figures. Their principle responsibility is to assure the safety of their passengers, for which they go through vigorous physical training. Then, consistent with the maintenance of standards of professional conduct, they provide high-quality customer service, involving complex food and beverage preparation and presentation.

The meeting with William Genoese, director of the Airline Division of the IBT, was scheduled at the Washington law firm of Verner Liipfert. Accompanied by Berl Bernhard, Verner Liipfert's managing partner, I waited for Genoese in a conference room. Genoese marched in, a bantam rooster of a man, with a retinue of approximately half a dozen rather large, burly men, none of whom spoke. He moved directly to the head of the table and, after a perfunctory handshake, proceeded to deliver a monologue. He described in great detail his experience with NWA and its management. He continued uninterrupted for approximately twenty minutes. Although he had started out in a calm voice, as he proceeded, he became increasingly overwrought by his own description of accumulated slights and injustices until, eyes bulging, he began screaming. Then, after the man to his right gestured and tapped his watch, Genoese abruptly stopped, excused himself, and left the room. I had not said a word since we shook hands.

As I paced the conference room floor, I chanced to look out the window to the sidewalk below. There was Genoese gesturing wildly in front of three television cameras. A few minutes later, he returned and reclaimed his place at the head of the table, but before he could speak, I asked, "What was that all about?" "Oh," he replied, "I told the news people the demands that I made from you." And then he proceeded to repeat them. "But you didn't say any of those things to me," I responded. "Yeah, I know, but I had to hurry to make the six o'clock news. I was going to tell you them later."

As dutifully presented in the news that evening, Genoese demanded special job security for flight attendants, restructuring of the airline's pay system, and the firing of Rothmeier. He added, "If he doesn't address our concerns, I'm against any acquisition."

As it was finally my turn to speak, I told him that we would not meet any of his demands. But I did repeat to him the same things I had said to the leaders of ALPA and the IAM: that we were managers and builders, that we hoped to expand the airline and position it as a global leader, and that we weren't going to fire anybody. Everyone would get a clean slate, including labor leaders.

Bill Genoese listened quietly and softened his rhetoric. He said that the flight attendants deserved better treatment than they had received. I agreed, and he vowed to work with us. From that point until his retirement, he was unflagging in his support for our efforts at NWA. We had the necessary endorsement from the Teamsters and could proceed.

Why did organized labor, which was institutionally opposed to leveraged transactions and possessed the readily acknowledged power to stop this one, give us their support? I believe that there were two reasons.

First, relations with the existing management had reached rock-bottom. This expressed itself as a hatred of Rothmeier that was palpable, but which I believe was more symbolic than personal. To labor, he was the embodiment of a culture of disrespect and distrust of the individual. At Northwest, managers seemed to feel their role was to scrutinize employees for rule infractions upon which to base cases for individual dismissal.

And there were a lot of rules. Managers liberally dispensed written warnings to employees by way of the dread Form PD-147, a citation issued like a traffic ticket that accumulated in the employee's personnel folder. One rule forbade people related by blood or marriage to work for NWA because management feared collusion. Later, when we dispensed with the forms and rescinded the rules forbidding relatives to work at NWA, midlevel managers asked what they should do, or more precisely how they could control the employees. I had two suggestions: First, continue to sneak up on them but try to find someone doing something right, and praise them for it. Second, don't try to "control" the employees—free them up to take control of themselves.

Northwest was like a dysfunctional family. The employees were its battered children. They wanted change so badly that they were willing to take their chances even with a leveraged acquisition.

The second reason I believe we earned organized labor's support was that we achieved personal credibility. We said what we believed and we did what we said. We did not over-promise, and we didn't pull our punches. When I told Bill Genoese that we would not meet any of his demands, the message was unambiguous. Although we had signed a merger agreement expressly not conditioned on signing a pilots' contract, we freely conceded to the pilots during our first meeting that they had the power to stop our closing. When I sketched out a vision for the future of Northwest and was asked how I could make it happen, I said truthfully that I could not. I said that no one person could create the company as described, but 40,000 people pulling together could and that we needed to pull the people at Northwest together.

People believed us because they wanted to believe us, and because we never gave them a reason not to. While the road ahead would have many unforeseen obstacles, we would continue to apply our principles consistently. Later, as industry circumstances became more difficult and Northwest teetered on the edge of insolvency, many employees would understandably lose confidence in us personally. But they kept working, perhaps reflexively, for the vision that we had described. In doing so, they took control of their own lives. All the employees—union leaders, management, and the line employees—joined to make the vision a reality. They had signed on with us because we gave them hope. They succeeded because they became a team.

We had won the approval of Northwest's board, been grudgingly favored by Northwest's management, achieved the support of the financial community, outmaneuvered the competition, and earned the trust of organized labor. Now all we had to do was take on the federal government.

The airline industry was deregulated in 1978, but it seemed someone forgot to tell the US government. With the exception of domestic route structuring and pricing, which are monitored under the general antitrust laws, nearly every other aspect of the US airline industry is governed directly by a specialized unit of the federal government. In the Senate, aviation falls under the jurisdiction of the Committee on Commerce, Science, and Transportation, specifically the Subcommittee on Aviation Operations, Safety, and Security. In the House, jurisdiction is maintained by the Committee on Transportation and Infrastructure, specifically its Aviation Subcommittee. The DOT directly and through the FAA supervises commercial aviation for the executive branch. Various state and local agencies, in particular designated local airport authorities, provide their own layers of governance. While each unit of government has its own often-contradictory view of aviation policy, all government is united in its view of airlines as a source of revenue. Airlines are the golden geese of federal and municipal finance.

The prospect of changing control of Northwest Airlines therefore attracted the attention of government at all levels: state, local, and federal—and at the federal level, both houses of Congress and the executive branch. The interest went beyond protecting a source of tax revenue. An airline the size of Northwest is an integral part of the country's transportation system, and thus an important public resource.

We can trace the settlement of our entire country to the evolution of transportation. First, the ships that brought the first European settlers to these shores. Then the bridges, canals, and turnpikes (for which the first corporate charters were granted), which allowed us to begin the penetration of our great interior landmass. Then the mighty railroads, a vast public/private venture, spanned our continent and integrated its diverse regions. These were followed in the 1950s by construction of the interstate highway system, which connected our cities and towns and made possible the extensive suburban development of our country.

Then we entered the jet age, ushering in an even greater period of national expansion and integration. The character of whole communities is reflected in their transportation links. To face the loss or substantial diminution of air transportation is a frightening prospect for any community.

Thus the proposed transfer of Northwest Airlines to private ownership in a leveraged transaction attracted great attention from government at all levels. Northwest operated large hub operations in Minneapolis–Saint Paul, Detroit, and Memphis that connected to hundreds of cities throughout the country. As the principal air carrier serving the north-central United States, many of these cities were exclusively dependent on Northwest for air service.

Legislation was proposed in North Dakota to block the sale of Northwest. Representative Byron Dorgan of North Dakota petitioned the DOT to stop the transaction. Representative James Oberstar of Minnesota, chairman of the House Aviation Subcommittee, called for an investigation by the Government Accounting Office. "We will be putting this under the microscope," he said. The powerful John Dingell, representative from Detroit and chairman of the House Energy and Commerce Committee, announced a hearing on airline acquisitions, and various senators and congressmen voiced interest in passing legislation to prevent the acquisition of airlines in leveraged transactions. The DOT also announced its intent to conduct a thorough fitness review, examining our capabilities to operate an airline and reviewing in detail our financial and ownership structure and strategic plans, as well as the competitive implications of our acquisition. Ominously, they singled out the involvement of KLM as meriting particular scrutiny.

I flew to Washington to make our case, which involved meeting with approximately twenty different representatives and senators, each with their own particular concerns depending upon what district or state they represented and on which committee they served.

Fatigue became my principal enemy. When I finally arrived to meet Representative James Oberstar, who was not only chairman of the House Aviation Subcommittee but represented the city of Duluth in northern Minnesota, I thought that I had suffered a stroke. I couldn't understand a word he was saying. It turned out he was speaking to me in Italian. I was so tired that I didn't recognize it. Later, I was to meet Wendell Ford, Oberstar's counterpart on the Senate side. He was on the floor voting, so I was ushered into his office, where I inadvertently fell asleep as I waited on his couch. When the senator found me, he was none too pleased by this breach of decorum. Our relationship never recovered.

Among the people I met was a congressman from Georgia, the minority leader of the House Aviation Subcommittee. I had never heard of him, but he had an extraordinary grasp of the issues we were facing, and at the end of our thirty-minute meeting, I said, "You're the smartest SOB I've met up here." His name was Newt Gingrich.

I passed my final congressional exam when I survived testifying before the House Energy and Commerce Committee, chaired by the formidable John Dingell, who also represented Detroit, Northwest's largest hub operation. Over time, I actually came to enjoy testifying before Congress. I found that if you were respectful but forceful and direct, Congress pretty much responded in kind.

The most important meetings that I would have were with the DOT. The Secretary of Transportation was Sam Skinner. To my admitted surprise, he and his staff were extraordinarily professional, responsible, and responsive. We were able to gain their approval of our transaction within a month and subsequently negotiated and structured a series of agreements that profoundly changed US and international aviation policy.

The DOT approved the initial KLM investment, which for the first time gave a foreign airline a 10-percent equity position in a US domestic carrier. Ultimately, they agreed to let foreign airlines own up to 49 percent of a domestic airline, enabling easier capital access for US carriers and facilitating progress toward one day creating a global airline.

Secretary of Transportation Sam Skinner approves
acquisition of Northwest Airlines

We later significantly reshaped international aviation policy, at least
over the Atlantic. We obtained in succession an Open Skies Agreement
between the United States and the Netherlands, which allowed any airline to fly to any city without restriction between our two countries (the
restriction against a foreign carrier flying within a country would still
prevail); and antitrust immunity, allowing us to merge our operations
across the Atlantic with KLM and form a true joint venture, whereby we
could operate as one integrated airline. Other airlines followed suit, as
did other countries.

The principal architect of these international agreements was
Michael Levine, former dean of the Yale School of Management, senior
official with the US Civil Aeronautics Board, and Northwest executive
vice president of marketing from 1992 to 1999. In addition to his achievements in the international arena, he also took the lead in developing a new
domestic strategy for Northwest in the mid-1990s. Northwest departed
from the industry doctrine of ubiquity (flying everywhere), instead

concentrating its route system around its fortress hubs and achieving industry-record profits. Other airlines subsequently followed our lead. Mike accomplished for airline marketing what I had for hotel finance.

Having obtained our regulatory approvals, we moved on to answer a question that I had inadvertently raised a month earlier: Would this be amateur night at the Roxie? The answer was anticlimactic; the syndication of the $3.6-billion bank loan was oversubscribed by two to one. We officially closed the acquisitions of Northwest Airlines on July 29, 1989, a frenetic six weeks after signing the merger document.

As I flew home to Los Angeles, the reverie of the big moment was quickly broken. The plane was filthy. The flight attendants looked dowdy in their cranberry-colored outfits. Service was terrible. The gate agent was surly. There was a lot to do that we hadn't done before. We would have to change a culture.

On September 26, I gave the keynote address at the annual Minnesota Chamber of Commerce Dinner. The banner headline in the *Star Tribune* read "Checchi Takes Off!" I started by saying that half the people in the Twin Cities must have asked, "What's a Checchi and where is it going?" The speech was very well received. We were off to a good start—or so it seemed. But I had no idea where I was going.

We had scheduled a big dinner and celebration at the Rainbow Room at Rockefeller Center in New York City. It was to be a thank-you event for all the people who had worked on the transaction, many of whom had never met each other. We included all the partners, the management of the company, and the union leaders and their spouses as a gesture that we were making a new beginning and looking to create a new culture at Northwest.

A few days before the dinner, on September 29, we were informed that we would be flying solo. Steve Rothmeier and four of his most senior executives announced they were pulling the releases on their golden parachutes and were leaving Northwest effective immediately. We prevailed on them to at least finish the week.

I don't think I need say what we thought of this lack of professionalism. Airlines may be the most complicated business in the world. The livelihoods of 40,000 people were directly tied to this one, as were the economic prospects of countless other businesses and whole communities. It seemed inconceivable, even unethical that Rothmeier and the other managers would abandon their responsibilities to their employees, community, and other corporate relationships. We had never planned to manage the business ourselves, only to serve on the board, finance and develop an expansion strategy, and help bridge the cultural chasm between labor and management.

Somewhere flying over Ohio en route to the closing party, as the partners grappled with the challenge of producing management succession for Rothmeier and his team, I became chairman and, by default, leader of an airline. Fred Malek agreed to become interim president until we recruited a full-time CEO. And Gary Wilson agreed to work his way out of Walt Disney and take direct responsibility for the finance and strategic planning functions. My life would never be the same. I was changing a lot more than places.

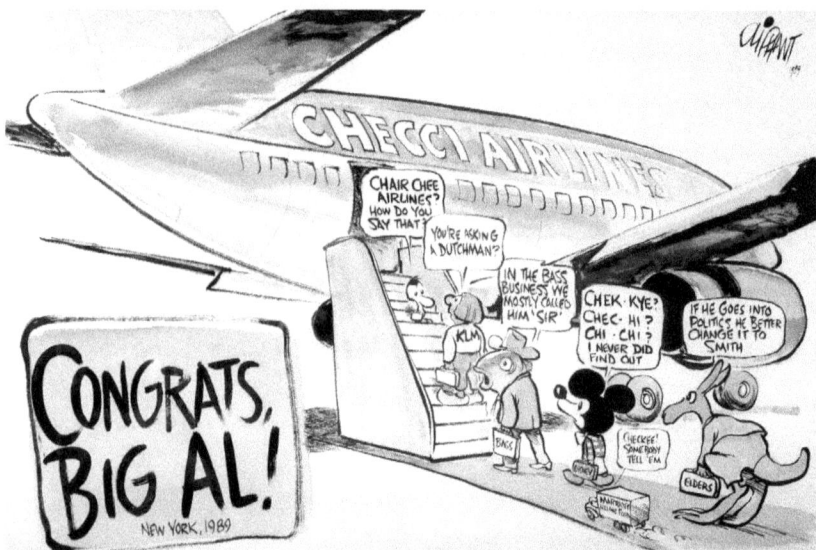

Surprise gift from attorney Berl Bernhard at the closing party.

Twelve

The Unfriendly Skies

They were nothing more than people, by themselves. Even paired, any pairing, they would have been nothing more than people by themselves. But all together, they become the heart and muscles and mind of something perilous and new, something strange and growing and great. Together, all together, they are the instruments of change.

Keri Hulme

WE HAD OUR MARCHING orders. Fred Malek would run the operations until we could find a full-time CEO, while I set about the task of changing the culture.

There was a formidable gulf between Northwest management and the employees. Communication had been one-way only: top to bottom. To begin reaching out, I decided from the outset that we would have to change the communication strategy. I would let the employees speak, and I would listen.

I went on a four-week barnstorming tour to all of Northwest's hubs and other cities with significant operations. We set up microphones: one for me, and several for the employees. Since flight attendants and pilots would be transiting throughout the day and all the employees were on shifts, we would hold as many as six meetings a day at a single site to get to as many employees as possible. The pilots union and the IAM also arranged for me to appear at large union meetings, where we would follow the same format.

Each session ran about ninety minutes. I would make a brief statement of introduction and a declaration of the goals that we had established: to make Northwest the best airline to fly for our customers; to make it the best place to work for employees; to be the best managed; and to be a great corporate citizen. I acknowledged the complexities of the business and that it was important to adhere strictly to certain procedures, but noted that it was also a service business, which meant that we had to be responsive and entrepreneurial. We intended to empower the employees to make decisions and to make mistakes. They only had to ask themselves three questions: Is this decision or action good for the customer? Is it good for my fellow employees? Is it good for the enterprise that has to support us? I stated that I would back any decision, recommendation, or change that could answer those questions affirmatively. Then I turned the meeting over to them.

The outpouring of feeling was enormous. First, there was extraordinary emotion and passion as these hardworking people detailed the genuine pain and disrespect that they had experienced in the workplace. Then there were expressions of embarrassment and shame that they could not deliver a better product to the customer. In all the meetings, I surprisingly never heard a complaint about salaries or benefits. People just wanted to be treated with respect, to be equipped to do a good job, and to have a sense of belonging and community.

All told, I flew to over fifty of Northwest's largest stations and met and talked with every employee that I could. On the planes I visited the cockpit so the pilots could tell me—yet again—how to run the airline, and I visited with all the flight attendants and pitched in to help them serve the customers. Everywhere I went, I received envelopes and notes from employees describing what was wrong and how to fix it.

The newspapers picked up on my tour from the employees. They said, "It's almost like a political campaign"; "It's a new era at Northwest." *Star*

Tribune columnist Jim Klobuchar wrote, "It took the bottom-line manuals a while to discover something that Checchi may have adopted by instinct: If you show people you trust them and need them, you're likely to have a more productive company than if you threaten them or ignore them. As a customer, I'm euphoric. I might even start checking my bags again." We got our message out fast, and people could see that we were listening. Now we had to show that we heard them. We had to deliver.

Airlines run on thin margins. The business is brutally price-competitive. You can't throw money at problems, but we had to take action. Out went the PD-147 and the antinepotism rules immediately. We changed the employee pass policy to allow more liberal flying privileges. We instituted employee recognition programs and awards. We redesigned employee uniforms to give them a more professional look. We announced nearly a half-billion-dollar investment in service improvements, including a battery of formal employee training programs in every facet of customer service. We revamped existing communication vehicles and instituted new ways to keep the employees informed. We set up committees involving line employees to address service and operational problems. We designed charitable programs where we raised money and donated money and services for the communities that we served. We even instituted the industry's first recycling program. All in all, we implemented over one hundred new policies and programs, many suggested by our employees, to help Northwest achieve the four objectives that I had stated in those initial meetings.

We also took dramatic steps to support the employees and manage the business better. Over the next two years, we replaced nearly all of the top fifty managers in the company. We made mistakes here, including a CEO replacement for Fred Malek who lasted less than two months, but we acted quickly to rectify them. But there was much for which I, at least, was unprepared.

Northwest had substantial operations in Asia. They required the same personal attention as the domestic operations. On December 5, 1989, it was reported in the news media that I had departed Manila. I had arrived three days earlier to meet with employees and inspect our freight operations, just a few hours before a military coup erupted to overthrow President Corazon Aquino. I was in the top floor of a hotel. Soldiers on the ground were exchanging fire with those on the roof above me. Although I was never in any real danger, I was unable to communicate with the United States for several days. When I finally got through to my daughter Kristin, I took full credit for saving the president of the Philippines. My daughter said, "Sure, Dad, probably the most heroic thing you did was order room service." How did she know?

On December 31, 1989, it was reported that Northwest jumbo jet Flight 51 from Paris landed in Detroit "uneventfully." Three days before, we had been alerted to a terrorist threat. It was recommended either that we cancel the flight, or keep quiet, do a thorough search of the plane, and if nothing was found continue the flight as scheduled. It was my call. I decided that instead, we would announce that a threat was made and give the passengers the option of rebooking, but that we could not buckle to terrorist threats; we would not cancel the flight. We flew the nearly empty plane as scheduled. We were applauded for the decision by the press as well as a victims' group established after the downing of Pan Am 103 by terrorists.

On March 8, 1990, three Northwest pilots were arrested for FUI (flying under the influence of alcohol). All three would be indicted, convicted, and receive jail terms. We could not undo the damage, but we could turn this into an opportunity to reexamine our policies. Northwest had a program for treating alcohol abuse. If the company suspected that a pilot had an alcohol problem, he would be automatically grounded for a minimum of two years. Rather than deter pilots from drinking, however, the result was that no pilot would admit to a problem and seek treatment.

We changed the policy to encourage pilots to seek help. Any pilot who came forward with a drinking problem would receive treatment at a special medical program at our expense and then, upon successful completion of it, be reinstated under a program of monitoring, interviewing, and testing. We had to endure about six months of Jay Leno jokes on national television, but the industry followed our lead to deal with this problem. Most importantly, our employees learned that we would take care of our own. On October 13, 1993, the *New York Times* reported: "Ex-Drunken Pilot Gets a Second Chance." The captain of the flight, having served his prison sentence and rehabilitated himself, was reinstated.

On Monday, December 3, 1990, a nightmare occurred. The *Pioneer Press* reported that a blinding fog, a wrong turn, and a flash fire left eight people dead at Detroit Metro when a Northwest jet, screaming toward takeoff, hit a second jetliner that had strayed onto its runway. An additional 191 passengers and crew members narrowly escaped death when the planes avoided head-on impact. But twenty-one of them were injured.

I had no experience with this kind of tragedy. The conventional wisdom, I was told, was to stay away. You are not supposed to let yourself become a spokesman or you'll become a target. I knew at once that I did not agree with that brand of advice. I thought that the person in charge of the airline should be there himself. I chartered a plane, and Kathy and I arrived in Detroit at four a.m. I went on CNN and accepted full responsibility and said that we would cooperate fully with the FAA investigation. We visited all the victims and their families and went to the hospital. One man was burned so badly he was wrapped in bandages like a mummy. All he could do was squeeze my hand. We talked to the pilots and consoled the employees. I later spoke at the funeral service of a Northwest flight attendant who had died in the accident.

The experience showed me that we were not as prepared to deal with the aftermath of an accident as we should have been. In the weeks following, we instituted a new crisis-management system for the US and Asian operations. I also asked the FAA to do a top-to-bottom investigation of our company and our systems to show that we were doing all that we could to ensure the safety of our passengers and employees.

As with the incident with the drinking pilots, we garnered positive support from outside. The *Star Tribune* reported, "When two Northwest airlines collided, killing 8, Checchi and his wife Kathy made a decision to fly to Detroit. On Tuesday Checchi visited 7 hospitalized passengers, met with crew members from the two planes and with other Northwest personnel in Detroit and held a difficult news conference. It was a stunning public relations success—because it was the appropriate thing to do.

Whatever the investigator's verdict on the crash and Northwest's culpability for it, Checchi's comportment in Detroit was outstanding. This is the way American business executives should behave. It's too rare that they do."

I also received an interesting inquiry from the Teamsters union. One of our flight attendants had been approached to appear in *Playboy* magazine. She wanted to know if this would affect her employment at Northwest. I tried to phrase an answer consistent with the message that we had been trying to convey to our employees. As the father of two daughters, I also ventured some advice:

Dear Nancy:

It has come to my attention that you are contemplating posing for a forthcoming issue of *Playboy* magazine. Through your union representative there have been inquiries about whether your future employment at Northwest would be impacted by your appearance in the magazine.

The short answer is that you may continue your employment at Northwest without prejudice provided that Northwest is not identified in any way in your portrayal and that you continue to perform your future duties in a manner consistent with company standards.

The decision to proceed with the magazine is yours, but I want you to consider a few things. We are all working hard to build Northwest. We are dedicated to making this a great company for our employees and our customers. We all have mutual responsibilities to one another. What one person does affects us all.

I believe that a company should stand for something—have values. Through our actions as well as our work we communicate those values. I think that you owe it to all of us to consider the possible effect on our efforts if one of our people poses in *Playboy*. What does it say about us?

On a personal note, I also ask you to consider your own circumstances. This may seem like a lark today, but you will have to live with this in the future. I urge you to consider the potential impact of this on possible future relationships with a husband or your children. Those pictures follow you for the rest of your life. What seems like a good idea today may not be so good in the years to come.

The ultimate decision, of course, is yours. That's as it should be. We want all of our employees to think for themselves and do what is right.

Good luck.

She made her own decision and passed on the photo shoot.

Perhaps the highlight of my first year at Northwest was being named a recipient of a Lifetime Achievement Award from the National Italian American Foundation (NIAF). The annual NIAF dinner is a black-tie event for 1,500 and a command performance for much of official Washington. My fellow honorees were quarterback Dan Marino and actor Alan Alda. Befitting an Italian banquet, the triple-tiered dais included about fifty people. I was seated in the front row with Congresswoman Connie Morella on my left and Supreme Court Justice Antonin Scalia on my right. One of the IAM national labor leaders came up, ignoring Morella, a Republican, to give me a double handshake: "Al, we're proud of ya; we're proud of ya." Then he turned to Scalia, poked a finger about four inches from his nose, and said, "And you; you're a disgrace to the Italians!" I thought I would fall on the floor.

But I gave probably the best speech of my life that night. Twenty years later, there are still people who come up to me and remember it, because I somehow found the words to express what it meant to immigrate and find a place for yourself and your family in this great country:

I actually gave thought to accepting this award tonight without making any public remarks. I know that all of you who are Italian Americans already understand what this honor means to me.

You understand the emotions that I feel as I share this moment with those most close to me—my wife and children, who are my continual support and inspiration. My parents, who each sacrificed so much of themselves to put me here tonight. Three sisters, who perhaps made the greatest sacrifices of all to support their big brother, the firstborn and only son in an Italian American household! My Uncle Vincent, who gave me my first job and set the course for my future career. And Aunt Lena, whose heart and kitchen were always open to me.

You who are Italian-Americans also know my thoughts about those not here tonight: four grandparents who got off the boat—uneducated, unable to speak English, but with a fierce pride and dedication to their children, and their adopted country.

You understand my particular feelings tonight about my grandmother, Dina Checchi, the matriarch of our family, who passed away only a few years ago, a woman who held husband and sons together through the Great Depression, ranged over two successive generations, and burned into each of us an indelible sense of personal identity and obligation.

You know, without having met them, my Uncle Al, Uncle Tony, Uncle Pusch, and Uncle Secondo. You know about the others, too—Zaita, Tonino, Sergio, Leilia, and Antoinette.

You know about the whole ménage of people—relatives, friends, acquaintances—as a child growing up, who knew who they all were—the greatest collection of people—all different, yet similar—all seemingly related—all making me feel important—like a son.

Italian-Americans understand all this. They have lived it.

But it occurs to me that not all of you here tonight are Italian Americans—fate has not been that kind to everyone! So let me offer you then at least some additional explanation of what this evening is all about.

First, if you don't know by now, it's all about family. When two Italian Americans get together, it is cause for a reunion—

whether they are related or not. Basically, you folks have been invited to a mass family reunion tonight.

It is also a celebration of a shared heritage. Being Italian American is about traditions, and the merging of two great national cultures.

This evening is about a process of individual struggle—each of us coming to grips with his cultural identity—simultaneously trying to change it and preserve it, to mask it, and to flaunt it.

Being Italian American is about participation, individual and collective, in the life and institutions of a country. We are what America is all about. It is about struggles and achievements in the past, and about dreams and aspirations for the future. It is about responsibility—to those who have preceded us and those who are to follow.

Being Italian American is also about things more tangible—like flesh, and blood, and muscle and sinew, and a coming to terms with the inevitable. Things with which my grandparents did not have to contend; things even my parents did not have to confront. But things that I and my children and my children's children must face.

You see, I married a non-Italian. A great lady—don't get me wrong—obviously lucky—she at least got to marry an Italian American! But Kathy has no Italian blood.

This deficiency in an otherwise perfectly fine woman raises for me, as it has for countless others, one of life's profoundest questions:

Are my children Italian?

My son, Adam, age thirteen (please stand up), was born with blonde hair, blue eyes, and fair skin—my God, he looks like a German! Fortunately, several years ago, when he was eight, he confronted his mother: "Mommy," he said *(gesturing with hands)*, "am I Italian? I know that Daddy is Italian—but am I Italian?" With hand gestures like that, I knew that I no longer had to worry about Adam.

Daughter Kristin, age eleven (up, up, Kristin)—look at her. Isn't she beautiful? Dark hair, dark eyes, dark skin, hot to the touch, and a fiery temper—I have never worried about Kristin.

Then Kate, five years old (stand on a chair, Kate)—my Kato—pink and white, blue eyes, and light brown hair—a problem? No, not Kate; even at an early age, she displays the temperament of a Mussolini!

So you see before you a man at peace with himself—I can safely say *(gesturing with hands)*, "My children are Italian!"

And tonight, it is with a profound sense of gratitude that I accept this honor that you have bestowed on me. On behalf of my grandparents, my parents, my sisters, my relatives, and near-relatives—we Italians don't just have friends—on behalf of all of those who have preceded me, and on behalf of my wife, my children, and my children's children, I thank you.

God bless you, and God bless America.

Looking back, it's hard to remember that there was a time when things were going well at Northwest and in the airline industry, but in May 1990, the *Pioneer Press* reported that 9to5, National Association of Working Women, would name me one of the year's five top bosses, based on my nomination by a Northwest flight attendant. A month later the same newspaper reported, "For customers and employees alike, it has been a year that far exceeded expectations. Workers rave that the future looks brighter for them and their company. Many passengers marvel that the carrier is on the upswing for service, turning around its once tainted reputation. Bank loans have been whittled back much faster than expected, and a new team of financial whizzes has been hired." Some misguided group even had CHECCHI FOR SENATE buttons produced. I still have mine along, with the later 1991 model: CHECCHI with a big red slash through it!

On August 2, 1990, the *New York Times* reported, "Iraqi troops crossed the Kuwait border today and penetrated deeply into the country and into

Kuwait's capital, senior Administration officials said. The United States condemned the invasion." This was the beginning of events in the region that would ultimately lead to the bankruptcy, liquidation, or merger of every major airline in America.

To put the economic effects of the Gulf War in perspective, at the time of the invasion, the price of jet fuel was 58 cents per gallon. The US airline industry was consuming 15 billion gallons of fuel per year at an annual cost just over $8.5 billion. The industry had never made more than $1.75 billion in any year. Fuel prices immediately started rising and peaked in October 1990 at $1.39 per gallon, an annualized price increase of over *$12 billion.*

Airline traffic and revenues also declined precipitously as travelers feared that the conflict could be extended to involve attacks on commercial airplanes. When America commenced its military response on January 16, domestic airline traffic declined nearly 15 percent; international traffic in some markets plunged as much as 50 percent.

Within the year, the industry imploded: Eastern Airlines, Midway Airlines, and Pan American Airlines disposed of most of their assets and liquidated. Trans World Airways, America West, and Continental Airlines declared bankruptcy. And scores of smaller airlines simply disappeared.

In the face of this economic cataclysm, we at NWA had only two possible responses, both of which proved ineffective but illustrative of the industry's and the country's problems.

Although every airline in America immediately began laying off workers to reduce costs, I decided to hold off. I went to labor, explained our situation, and said we had a chance to do something different. If everyone took a temporary 10-percent pay cut, we would take care of our own and not lay off anyone. Some labor leaders were willing to consider it, but it would have to be unanimous among labor groups. Unfortunately, they seemed to distrust each other more than they distrusted us, and we could not get unanimity. The proposal died and we, too, had to lay off about 5 percent of our people.

I testified before Congress and made the case that the industry was clearly a war casualty. Recognizing this, I pointed out that other countries had taken remedial actions to alleviate some of the economic pressure on their airlines. The US airline industry was paying 8 percent of its revenues as a ticket tax, which vastly exceeded its profits even in the best of years. I suggested that the government loan the money back to the airlines for a year until things stabilized. Congress saw it differently. Their attitude was "It's our money, and you also have to help pay for the war." The tax was increased to 10 percent, and a new tax, the Passenger Facility Charge of two to four dollars per passenger, was added to provide for airport improvements. At a time when airlines were hemorrhaging cash, these taxes and fees added several billion dollars to annual airline costs. So much for my talents as a lobbyist.

The Gulf War came to an end in the spring of 1991. Several airlines had liquidated and many others were restructuring in bankruptcy. The entire industry was weakened. At Northwest, the capitalization that we had put together to acquire the company had withstood the unanticipated effects of war. Our employees had performed superbly. We were starting to get recognition for our service improvements, and the new management that we had put in place was making us more efficient. We were also doing a better job of scheduling and pricing to find new revenue opportunities. We were shaken but still standing, and with the passing of war clouds we saw a glimmer of daylight.

When we acquired Northwest Airlines, we inherited a large order of aircraft to be built by France's Airbus Industries. Delivery of the planes would start in 1991 and extend over several years. Because Airbus technology was unique, a new type of maintenance facility had to be built to service the planes when their first overhauls were required in 1994.

Many communities across the country were anxious to host the new maintenance facilities and their $100-million annual employee payroll. They offered extensive financial inducements, such as free land, cash subsidies, tax abatements, and job credits. Previous Northwest management, perpetually at odds with the Minnesota press, government, and the Twin Cities community, had announced that the bases would be built outside of Minnesota at a location to be determined.

I had set as one of our objectives good corporate citizenship. When the governor of Minnesota asked if I would reconsider locating the bases in Northwest's home state, I agreed, but only if Minnesota's terms were competitive financially with the offers we were receiving from other states and municipalities. On April 8, 1991, I received a financial proposal from the state of Minnesota. It was elaborately presented, with a laminated facing page signed by the governor, the majority and minority leaders of the Minnesota State Senate and House of Representatives, and Congressman James Oberstar, chairman of the House Aviation Subcommittee of the US Congress. It appeared that Minnesota wanted the bases, and they were prepared to pay to get them.

For constitutional and other reasons, Minnesota could not grant an outright subsidy, but they could loan money at their cost of borrowing. Since this was considerably below our cost as an airline, it was agreed that we would calculate the value of their proposal to be the interest that we would save from borrowing from the state versus borrowing from private financing sources. We negotiated a deal whereby we would borrow some $740 million from the state. That would be worth around $20 million in annual interest expense savings to us, which was competitive with the other proposals that we had received. Finalization of the deal required the consent of the Minnesota legislature, which I took to be *pro forma*. This proved to be the most naïve action of my business career and almost destroyed Northwest Airlines.

Throughout the ensuing nine months, we were caught up in the intramurals of Minnesota politics. In the hands of politicians, the bipartisan transaction that *they* had presented to us was distorted into a "bailout" that *we* were requesting from them. In the no-holds-barred political fight that followed, the reputation of the company was so damaged by misinformation that its credit relationships were severely threatened. Throughout this episode, I was the point man and focal point of ire. Like it or not, I was the face of Northwest, and before this was over, I was transformed by political foes of the transaction into a wolf—literally.

As part of the legislative process, I was requested to appear before a joint session of the Minnesota legislature, which I was told was a first.

STATE OF MINNESOTA

OFFICE OF THE GOVERNOR
130 STATE CAPITOL
SAINT PAUL 55155

ARNE H. CARLSON
GOVERNOR

April 8, 1991

Mssrs. Gary Wilson
  and Alfred Checchi
Co-Chairmen
Northwest Airlines, Inc.
Minneapolis/St. Paul International Airport
St. Paul, MN 55111

Gentlemen:

We are pleased to present a joint-state offer to construct a major heavy maintenance facility for Northwest Airlines' A-320 aircraft, located at the Duluth International Airport. This project would be financed through three tax-exempt revenue issues backstopped by state and local direct and indirect obligations. We believe this proposal represents the lowest effective cost to Northwest and will support significant job creation by one of Minnesota's major employers.

We would welcome an early opportunity to review this proposal in detail and respond to any questions which you might have.

Sincerely,

Arne H. Carlson
Governor

John Fedo
Mayor, City of Duluth

Roger Moe
Senate Majority Leader

Robert Vanasek
Speaker of the House

Duane Benson
Senate Minority Leader

Terry Dempsey
House Minority Leader

James Oberstar
Congressman, 8th District

William Kron, Chairman
St. Louis Board of Commissioners

Wayne Dalke, Commissioner
IRRRB

Hugh Schilling, Chairman
Metropolitan Airports Commission

AN EQUAL OPPORTUNITY EMPLOYER
PRINTED ON RECYCLED PAPER

Proposal from the governor and leadership of Minnesota legislature

I explained the purpose of the bases, their anticipated costs, and the number of employees that would be required to operate them. I made no claims for benefits to Minnesota; I merely stated that the deal that

Minnesota had offered us was "generous, comprehensive, professional, and quite attractive."

In retrospect, aside from the angst that was created for the financial community and our employees, what followed was truly amusing. A meeting with State Senator Charlie Berg had a memorable beginning:

"Mr. Checchi, I think you are a lousy businessman."

"Why do you say that, Senator?"

"You ordered those planes and you hadn't built the maintenance sheds."

"That's correct, Senator. We don't need them for another two and a half years."

"Well, I'm a pig farmer. And I want you to know that when I buy pigs, I've already built the pens."

Here I was, left speechless again.

Senator Gene Merriam was quoted in the newspaper, comparing me to the fast-talking conman Professor Harold Hill: "He's like the Music Man, and we're going to end up with the band uniforms." I took exception to this until Kathy pointed out I was a little like Professor Harold Hill: After all, I had talked her into marrying me! She was not so cavalier, however, when another state official said, "He comes in there and he's wearing those flashy clothes, has that flashy smile, and he's got his flashy wife." My dignified wife, lawyer, and mother of three nearly had to be peeled off the ceiling. Another state politician said, "Al Checchi couldn't sit on the bar stools where I go. He would slip right off." I was alternately described as a "leech," a "parasite," and—a personal favorite—a "mugger in Gucci shoes."

Thanksgiving Day was the best or worst, depending on the thickness of your skin. As I opened the newspaper, always an adventure in Minnesota during that period, there was a full page drawing of a snarling wolf with dollar bills dripping from his mouth. The caption: "The Wolf Is at Your Door—His Name Is Al." I gave it to Kathy and wished her "Happy Thanksgiving!"

We finally closed the deal on December 17 and got exactly what we had bargained for nearly nine months earlier. My only public comment on all the attention that I had received was to quote my fourteen-year-old son: "Gee, Dad, you'd think you were the only guy in the state who owns a car, gets a haircut, and wears a suit." I expect that the irony was lost on them, but I enjoyed the hell out of it.

The infamous wolf ad

At the dawn of 1992, though the scars from the tumultuous previous months were still visible, there was a general feeling that the worst days had passed and the industry would begin to rebound. "The good news for airlines," the *Pioneer Press* predicted on January 2, 1992, "is that 1992 will be better than 1991."

The situation at Northwest did, indeed, seem somewhat brighter at the start of the year. Though a great deal of energy had been expended on steering the company through the Gulf crisis, Northwest had, as the *New York Times* pointed out on March 6, 1992, a number of competitive advantages. "Under Checchi and Wilson," Eric Berg wrote, "labor relations, punctuality, and overall level of passenger service have improved; the company has met all of its debt obligations and its Pacific Route system remains the envy of the industry . . ."

However, nothing could have prepared us—or the industry—for "Hurricane Bob."

Bob Crandall, CEO of American Airlines, the world's largest, was about to impose his "final solution" for the industry he aspired to dominate. A 1990 *New York Times Magazine* article said it all: "His lean, wiry body encased in camouflage fatigues, a bandanna around his forehead and a toy plastic rifle in hand, Robert Crandall burst onto the video screen. In his film debut at the 1987 meeting in Fort Worth, the American Airlines chief appeared as Crando, the terror of the competition, the unstoppable killing machine of the airline wars. The Rambo guise eloquently reflected both Crandall's macho business style and his vaunting ambition. . . . These days American Airlines executives are reluctant to discuss the tape, much less show it. Crando, the feeling seems to be, was going a little too far . . ." Or as Crandall described himself, "My friends call me Mr. Crandall; my enemies call me Fang."

On April 9, 1992, as reported in the *Wall Street Journal*, "American Airlines introduced a novel four-tier fare program yesterday that lowers its top fares by as much as 50 percent and by day's end, almost every major US airline had climbed onto its bandwagon." Then, most ominously, "American's bold move toward a simplified air-fare structure will shave as much as $100 million off of second quarter revenues, the company said . . ."

No one minded simplifying revenues, but American Airlines CEO Bob Crandall set prices below costs. Crando was raining napalm on his own position. He had built a Ponzi-like scheme that was unsupportable. He had persuaded his employees to accept a lower wage, B-scale, for new hires that fueled short-term capacity expansion. Over time, when the wages paid B-scale employees converged and caught up with the old scale, Americans' costs increased. It would have to force out competition to support the artificially high capacity it had acquired.

On April 20, 1992, *USA Today* reported Carl Icahn of TWA's charge that American was cutting fares to force the nation's weaker carriers out of business. On ABC's *This Week*, David Brinkley said, "You believe in the tooth fairy if you believe these fares won't go up." Crandall, on the same program, said they were not meant to destroy weaker airlines but to "expand the market." *Time Magazine* reported: "There is a darker side to the fare wars: Many experts see it as a thinly veiled declaration of war against low-cost rivals like TWA and Continental . . ." Standard and Poors warned that even nonbankrupt major carriers would find it more difficult to pay off their debts. It put all carriers on its credit watch list.

On May 19, 1992, the *Wall Street Journal* reported that the much-trumpeted simplification of airfares didn't appear to be creating as much new business as some travel executives had hoped. The *Star Tribune* reported on June 1: "American's brutal fare war is a bid to dominate airline pricing, deal a body blow to healthy competitors and perhaps kill off an ailing carrier or two." Kemper Securities Group analyst Dan Hersh said, "Now it's a war of balance sheets. We're going to find out who has the most cash to last." In June, *USA Today* reported that Crandall had faced his accusers in a crowded Senate room and told them to stop complaining. "I don't decide who is in the airline business. I don't like being described as a villain." America West CEO Michael Conway countered, "In my opinion, there is a predator loose, and that predator is American."

The entire industry was hemorrhaging cash. Northwest's solvency was threatened. We would first have to stop the American Airlines assault and then deal with the damage that it had created. We initially countered the American Airlines price reductions by introducing even lower prices of our own. In this way we sought to make it so expensive for American to control pricing that even Crandall could not afford to fight the war much longer. We then joined a major lawsuit filed by Continental Airlines and America West against American. The consequences of losing the suit would have been bankruptcy for American Airlines. We hoped to put pressure on the American board to rein in "Crando." By midsummer the war ended. American abandoned Value Pricing. We then had to deal with the war's aftermath.

Because American had destroyed the financial underpinning of the industry, new lenders were reluctant to invest in the industry and refinance the debt that was coming due. Our existing lenders indicated a willingness to consider refinancing, but only if we could reduce our costs to conform to the present difficult economic circumstances of the industry and get other creditors to stretch out their payments, too. We had already drawn down all of our cash reserves. Without an additional infusion, we would be out of cash by the end of the year.

Unless we were to go the route of most of our competitors and declare Chapter 11, we would have to restructure Northwest Airlines outside of bankruptcy, a mammoth and unprecedented undertaking. All airlines were reducing head count and slashing expenses. We would do the same, but unless we could also negotiate labor-wage concessions, we could not achieve the $300-million-per-year cost reductions that the banks would minimally require to restructure our debt. We designed a bold plan to restructure Northwest Airlines outside of bankruptcy.

Gary Wilson managed negotiations with all the lenders and suppliers. In addition to working out a refinancing schedule acceptable to the hundred-bank syndicate, he negotiated terms with Northwest's largest creditors. These were tortuous discussions involving the treatment of deposits and credits for billions of dollars of scheduled aircraft and engine deliveries from Boeing, Airbus, General Electric, and Pratt & Whitney. Only the Armadillo could have pulled this off, and I awarded him Most Valuable Player for what we collectively achieved.

John Dasburg had joined us from Marriott Corporation a few years earlier as chief financial officer and then president and CEO of Northwest. He was responsible for running the airline day to day, a difficult job under the best of circumstances but incredibly challenging under these. He had to reduce headcount and costs while maintaining the operating integrity of the airline. Most importantly, he had to inspire, motivate, and provide reassurance to Northwest's employees through a period of great uncertainty. Under his leadership, Northwest achieved some of its best operating performance during the next year, and the employees stuck by us and participated in the restructuring.

I had the job of designing and negotiating the concession package with our unions and equity partners, who were all required to contribute to a solution judged equitable by all. As in the maintenance-base negotiation with the state of Minnesota, I was the public face of Northwest—there was no escaping this, and no one else wanted the job. I made no public statements, explanations, or excuses, however. I simply did my best.

The restructuring of Northwest was highly contentious and took a little over a year, stretching from the first presentations that we made to our employees in May 1992 until the pilots union finally agreed to a new contract at the eleventh hour on July 6, 1993. During this period, the national press held a death watch over Northwest. We were a constant source of reporting and speculation. There were several moments when all seemed lost, but the constituents of Northwest finally came together: labor, management, capital, as well as the local communities. It was a wrenching experience for all concerned. I avoided public comment, content for others to tell the story about how *they* saved the airline. The *New York Times* did record one quote—from the note card that I kept in the top drawer of my desk. It was from Abraham Lincoln:

> If the end brings me out all right, what is said against me won't amount to anything. If the end brings me out wrong, ten angels swearing I was right would make no difference.

Kathy used to joke that years in the airline business were like "dog years"—for every year in the industry, you aged seven. I arrived at Northwest Airlines a young man; I was no longer young. When it appeared that Northwest might also succumb to the financial pressures of the industry, I had promised to do my best to steer it to safe harbor. I wrote a letter to my son on April 30, 1993, when I was unsure how the Northwest voyage would turn out. I lost my innocence in Minnesota:

> There is a literary movement called Existentialism, one of whose major figures was the French author Jean-Paul Sartre. He wrote a play called *No Exit* in which three characters sit in an anteroom of Hell waiting to be admitted and thereby waiting for the suffering to start. As the three characters begin to interact, it becomes apparent that they have tremendous capacities to inflict pain upon one another. In death as in life, each is dependent upon others not only for companionship, but to achieve a sense of self. We are to a degree what others reflect us to be. At the end of the play as the characters create greater misery for each other, it becomes obvious that they are not going to move into another room, that they are already in Hell, and that they are their own tormentors.
>
> It occurs to me as it undoubtedly was intended by Sartre that Heaven or Hell exists right here on Earth, not necessarily in an afterlife, and that we are our own best angels or demons. There really are good people and bad as there are people who share goodness with others or afflict others with their evil.

The restructuring of Northwest was a success for all concerned. Northwest became the most profitable airline in the United States for the three years following the restructuring, even without the effects of the wage concessions. It went public in 1994. The employees who invested an average of 12 percent of their wages received common stock that at its high was worth approximately three times their concessions.

All the lenders and suppliers were repaid their full principal and interest. KLM became part of the world's most comprehensive airline alliance, which eventually enabled it to combine with Air France and form the largest airline in Europe. All the investors made exceptional returns. My personal holdings reached a value of over $700 million.

For several years, the Harvard Business School set aside up to three days and reviewed a battery of twelve cases on Northwest Airlines as the culminating exercise of the first-year MBA program. Union leaders, Minnesota politicians, and Northwest management participated in the class discussions.

Northwest had reached safe harbor.

The Northwest acquisition generated significant press coverage.

Early Northwest Plane.

Gov. speaking and Cong. Oberstar
at Airbus maintenance base signing.

How Quickly public opinion
can change.

Speaking at dedication of new Detroit terminal. President Clinton reacts.

PART III

THIRTEEN
Twice Blessed

Death be not proud, though some have called thee
Mighty and dreadfull, for, thou art not so,
For, those, whom thou think'st, thou dost overthrow,
Die not, poore death, nor yet canst thou kill me.

John Donne

As THE MARINE CORPS orchestra struck up "Hail to the Chief," I squeezed Kathy's hand and gave her the thumbs up. We had made it to the White House. It was April 2, 1996, and we were attending President Clinton's state dinner honoring Oscar Luigi Scalfaro, the president of Italy.

Wherever you are in the American social or political pecking order, a state dinner is the thrill of a lifetime. The intimate White House State Dining Room can seat only 180 guests at its tables of ten each. As we mingled during the cocktail hour among the other guests, many of them Italian Americans, I overheard more than one say what I was thinking: "If only my grandmother could see me now."

After escorting Kathy through the president and first lady's receiving line, I took my assigned place at the table in the front of the room to the left of the podium. A few minutes later I met my dinner partner,

First Lady Hillary Rodham Clinton. She was bright, extremely gracious, and a lot of fun. At the completion of dinner, as the other guests retired for music and dancing, Kathy and I excused ourselves and headed to the airport, where I boarded a chartered plane.

I had previously accepted an invitation from the Commerce Department to participate in a foreign trade mission. Departure from Washington was scheduled for April 1. When the invitation to the state dinner came a few weeks later, I inquired if I might take private transportation at my own expense and meet the other participants in the mission a day later.

Nine hours later, as the pilots prepared to make our final approach, we were contacted by air traffic control. "There is danger on the ground; abort and fly to a neutral country." It was only after I landed in Zurich, Switzerland, that I learned that the plane that I would have been on, the one carrying Secretary of Commerce Ron Brown along with thirty-four others, had crashed into a mountain at our original destination of Dubrovnik. All on board had perished.

This was the second time that fate had inexplicably intervened and spared me. I spent a solitary night thinking about my life and all the events that had led me to that point and place. Long ago I had set my course: I would pursue a private-sector career, hopefully achieve some useful experience and a degree of recognition, and then, at around age fifty, do public service in some appointed capacity. This had been the established pattern that produced the Roosevelt "brain trust," as well as the so-called "best and the brightest" that had heeded the call to serve in the Kennedy administration of my youth.

I had not reckoned that my career would include the extraordinary experience of going through the crucible of the Northwest saga or that I would ever amass the independent personal wealth that my various activities, particularly those on behalf of Northwest, would produce. At Northwest, I had dealt with a large cross-section of institutions: governments at all levels, local, state, federal, and foreign; organized labor at the local and national levels; and the fourth estate, the press, locally, nationally, and internationally.

I had led a complex, multifunctioned, quasi-public institution through a geopolitical crisis, structured and negotiated an unprecedented accord with organized labor, and similarly negotiated and guided to passage legislation, agreements, and even treaty changes with state, federal, and international legislatures and executive agencies. I had persisted and endured under adverse circumstances, intense pressure, and public scrutiny, and achieved my objectives. I had met my fiduciary responsibilities to all my constituencies. I had become, in my own terms, a leader.

These experiences, as well as the wholly unexpected windfall of accumulated personal wealth, enabled me to entertain the thought that, despite the road I had chosen to travel, maybe the two paths would converge. I could pursue a private-sector career and also run for high political office. I had been thinking about this for months after Northwest reached safety and returned to public ownership, since my job there was effectively complete.

I didn't sleep during that long night in Zurich. But I emerged in the morning newly resolved. With her permission, Kathy and I would change places once again, but this time she wouldn't have to move. I would run for governor of our home state, California.

FOURTEEN
The Long March

If I am not for myself, who will be for me?
If I am for myself only, what am I?
And if not now, when?

Rabbi Hillel

MONTHS BEFORE MY ABORTED flight to Dubrovnik, I began thinking about running for governor of California and set down three questions:

1. Am I qualified to be a political leader; has my past experience prepared me for such a public role?
2. Is knowledge about the economy and industry relevant to shaping public policy and managing public institutions; is there a symbiotic and mutually dependent relationship between the private and public sectors?
3. Does the office of governor of California have the power to affect change; can I develop a strategy to address the serious problems of America's most populous and complex state?

In a 1991 speech to the League of Minnesota Cities, a group of elected and appointed government officials, I had summarized my thoughts about leadership in the private and public sectors, and, in effect, answered my first question:

> All of us are involved in a common endeavor—serving the needs of the public. Managing and motivating large numbers of people is the same for all large institutions, public or private; the management of these institutions is essentially a political task, requiring us to balance the needs of many and varied constituent groups.
>
> As stewards over large amounts of society's resources, we share common responsibilities. Ours are positions of sacred trust; what we do is important. It really matters that we use these resources wisely, efficiently, and honestly.

I then went about explaining my views of management, which I felt should apply to leaders of all types of institutions:

> First, I believe that an individual can make a difference. Even in a large bureaucracy, you don't have to accept the status quo; you can be an agent of change.
>
> Second, I believe that people want leadership. In *Escape from Freedom*, the social psychologist Erich Fromm postulated that men have a fundamental fear of isolation. They are willing to trade some of their individuality in order to belong to something larger than themselves, whether it is family, a neighborhood, a corporation, a city, or a country.
>
> Third, I believe that success most often comes through simplicity. Business and public administration, like most endeavors, are basically common sense.
>
> Fourth, I believe that people respond better to inspiration and encouragement than fear. Trust breeds trust and loyalty breeds loyalty.

I then hazarded some advice:

> Public and private institutions face the same constraints—too much to do, too little to do it with. Insist on efficiency. Continually seek ways to reduce the costs of what you do.
>
> Empower all your employees to be decision-makers. The best ideas come from down low in the organization, where the rubber meets the road. Every employee has the power to create, to contribute something of value.
>
> In managing people, manage down, not up. Take care of the people under you and don't worry about the people over you.
>
> As leaders, seize responsibility, don't avoid it. Encourage accountability for the quality and efficiency of all your undertakings. Create an atmosphere where people feel they can dare to make a mistake.
>
> Most importantly, bring people together. We all must dedicate ourselves to repairing an increasingly frayed social fabric. Create a sense of shared participation and people will do great things.

With regard to the second question, in mid-March, a few weeks before my aborted flight to Dubrovnik, I had unsuccessfully submitted for publication to the *New York Times* an opinion piece concerning the relationship among the public and private sectors and the individual. I consider the private sector so important to the formation of public policy that I can't see how anyone could propose to lead government without either extensive private-sector experience of their own or, at minimum, an assembled team with significant and diverse business experience:

> A significant transformation of individual and institutional relationships is underway, and we require a better understanding of their sustainable capacities.
>
> In a system of democratic capitalism such as ours, there is no preset division between private and public sectors; there is no constitutionally protected right of private production. When

market forces fail to yield a desirable mix of goods and services, society shifts a greater share of economic activity to government. In the 1920s, the private sector accounted for 90 percent of GDP; today it accounts for less than 70 percent.

This shift of resources to government has not come without costs. Since market forces determine optimal production and impose efficiency in the private sector, and government is generally immune to the market, it is inherently less efficient.

In government, production is determined arbitrarily and resource allocation is coerced through taxation, regulation, or eminent domain. Expanding the public sector has accordingly caused less choice, and less freedom.

It is time for political leaders to rethink and redefine government's role. We must restrict government to achievable ends unobtainable through the free market, thereby freeing up resources for individual initiative and realizing the full productive potential of a free society.

But we don't just need a change in public policy. Corporate leaders must also step up to their responsibilities. If part of the problem is that business was shortsighted and created the conditions for government to expand, then an essential part of the solution is for business to take a wider and longer view of its role and purposes.

It's not just corporations and government that have to change. Our citizens will have to change, too, and take charge. In America, the individual is the fundamental political unit, not the state or the corporation. Institutions as such are only abstractions, inert and value-neutral. The only thing that animates them is us.

So we as citizens need to assert ourselves and demand a more limited role of government, where it does only what it can do well. We as consumers need to demand a more responsible private sector, capable of filling a wider role.

In the era we are now entering, public opinion can be instantly mobilized. Technology, the Internet, and the entire

communications revolution, rather than making people powerless, as Orwell suggested, will permit them to join together and
act together.

Change is here, and we cannot repeal it. Government must
become smaller and more efficient. Corporations need to broaden
their perspectives to encompass more fully and fundamentally
their obligations to society at large. Citizens and consumers must
take up the new tools of a new era to empower themselves and
transform the private as well as the political landscape.

There is an intimate relationship between the public and private sectors and their responsibilities to the individual citizen. My experience
as a change agent and leader in the private sector prepared me well for
public service.

However, if I was going to run for and possibly serve in public office,
it would only be with the purpose of making fundamental changes. I had
never been a caretaker in any previous capacity, and it didn't take much
to see that California had to reverse its trajectory. As for the third question, I had been thinking about the challenges facing California for years.
I began a systematic analysis to determine if I could mount an effort to
address them and make a meaningful difference.

I commenced by doing my own research: mostly reading about
California history, government structure, the constitutional powers of
the governor, and articles about specific issues like schools, water, and
transportation. I then widened the effort to include consultation with
several history and government professors from the California university system, as well as others involved with California government. As I
studied its recent political and economic history, it was evident to me that
something radical would have to be done to change California's direction. The Golden State, which had led the country during the twenty-
five years after World War II, had since experienced a precipitous linear
decline in every measure of civic health.

After I returned from Dubrovnik, I began assembling an issues team
that soon grew to ten people. Eventually we drafted a detailed strategic

plan that I felt could turn the state around. We summarized that strategy in a ninety-page book for distribution to the public, *The Checchi Plan: A Vision for California in the Twenty-First Century.* The plan placed particular emphasis on restructuring and decentralizing the public education system, which had deteriorated so much over the past several years. Education had been critical to my family's advancement. In a technology-driven society, it seemed more important than ever.

The plan addressed the need to revitalize the economy by referencing the symbiotic relationship existing between the public and private sectors and recommending the regulatory changes and infrastructure improvements required to stimulate economic development again in California.

It also targeted the need to restructure and repurpose government itself. Government was the only major institution in our society that had failed to change to meet the needs of a changing environment. Structures largely developed at the turn of the previous century were unsuited to meet the challenges of the twenty-first century.

To me, the numbers were indisputable: California was headed to insolvency. I concluded that unless we instituted fundamental changes of the type I recommended, the state would soon reach a point where it was unsalvageable. At that point, it wouldn't matter who led California. There would be no traditional way out. It would ultimately have to seek some kind of judicial restructuring. I frequently said of the immediacy of the election, "This is the last helicopter out of Saigon."

While this may not sound like the positive message that campaign consultants craft, I believed it to be the truth. We had made changes to avoid court intervention at Northwest, and we could do it here in California. Further, I was confident that a place as blessed with the human and material resources of California, while not as easy a fix as Walt Disney, could, with sound leadership and a well thought-out strategy, turn itself around and resume its positions of leadership in less than a decade.

The governor of California had the power to make over 2,500 appointments. There was ample constitutional authority and opportunity for an executive to have great impact on the future of America's most populous state.

Once I was satisfied that there was a job to do and I felt that I could do it, it was time to determine if I had any chance of getting it.

Could I win a gubernatorial race in California? More specifically, could I crash the party (any party), circumvent the interest groups that dominate the primary nominating process, and defeat the entrenched political careerists who kept this largely a private game?

My fate was already cast with respect to the party nomination for which I would have to contend. Shortly before I left Fort Worth, I had decided that I ought to register with one of the two major political parties. I had always voted for the person that I thought would do the best job and had cast as many Democratic ballots as Republican. As the two parties appeared to have different philosophies and directed their appeals to different audiences, I felt that it was time to at least nominally choose sides. I went about a due-diligence process, much as I would in analyzing an investment or a new career opportunity. I attended both Republican events and Democratic ones.

I quickly learned that regardless of the party, unless you were a candidate or one of the myriad people who make a career out of managing and working on campaigns (the best route to serving as staff for the victors), the sole interest of a political party in someone like me was as a campaign contributor. No one really cared about your ideas.

As I looked carefully at the two parties, I thought they were both flawed. In general, I found the Democrats irresponsible fiscally and hopelessly idealistic. They were indiscriminate. If the end was "good," they wanted to pursue it, irrespective of the practicality of the means. The Republicans that I met I found exclusionary and reactionary. They liked things the way they were or the way they thought things once had been, and seemed always to be looking backward or protecting the status quo. More often than not, both served up unworthy candidates, making elections a choice between the lesser of two poor alternatives. I continue to this day to cast my votes irrespective of party.

Given my family history, I believed in the importance of government as a guarantor of opportunity, favored assimilation and inclusion, and believed that change is inevitable. This pushed me toward the Democrats.

On the other hand, I believed that resources were finite, choices have to be made, and that commitment to limited government and maximum personal liberty are fundamental. This said Republican. I wished I could have the best of both, but I had to choose.

I made the decision, with little commitment to partisanship, to affiliate with the Democratic Party based on what I glibly stated at the time: "I think it is easier to teach economics to Democrats than compassion to Republicans." I would later find through experience that this was probably unfair to Republicans and overly generous to Democrats.

In November 1996, I surveyed my prospects for winning the primary and then the general election for governor of California. The primary would not take place for another nineteen months, on June 2, 1998—so I would have ample time to mount a campaign. The governor at the time, Republican Pete Wilson, was termed out. I would not have to run against an incumbent, which would be an advantage. Further, Wilson had played on California's ethnic divisions in fashioning his 1994 reelection campaign, and the acrimony that he had generated among all ethnic groups was still strong so that 1998 would probably be a Democratic year.

The competitive situation within the Democratic Party would be tricky. The sole announced Democratic candidate was the political careerist Lieutenant Governor Gray Davis. Davis was known as a plodding speaker and prodigious fund-raiser (it was quipped that he attended the opening of every door). He was closely tied to the major interest groups that supported the Democratic Party, but was an object of ridicule among much of the political press and many political insiders. Given his liabilities, I had a reasonable chance to defeat him, particularly in a one-on-one race.

Two other Democrats were prominently discussed: former congressman and current chief of staff to the president Leon Panetta, and Senator Dianne Feinstein. I liked Panetta and frankly thought that he would make a pretty good governor. Feinstein had lost to Pete Wilson in the 1990 race for governor, but as an incumbent senator and former standard-bearer for the Democratic Party in a previous gubernatorial race, she would have a lock on the nomination, no matter who else ran. I could only watch and wait to see how events would unfold.

In November 1996, California voters passed two state initiatives that could recast the electoral landscape and significantly improve my chances. First, the 1998 gubernatorial primary would be "open." This meant that Republicans and Democrats would for the first time run together, with the top two vote-getters winning the nomination. Independents, who had been previously excluded, could now also vote in the primaries. Theoretically, a nontraditional candidate like me might pull a few Republican votes; and if any appreciable number of newly eligible Independents chose to participate, I might have some advantage with them, too.

The second change was far more significant: Californians voted to impose campaign finance limits. Instead of the unlimited contributions that had turned California elections into special-interest auctions, no single individual or institution could contribute more than $500 to a candidate. There would, however, be no limits on what a candidate could contribute to himself.

This was a potential game-changer. It would not deter Dianne Feinstein, whose husband had independent wealth. It would, however, mean that Leon Panetta would have to declare his candidacy and start fund-raising soon to amass any appreciable war chest. And Gray Davis's strongest qualification for mounting a candidacy, his ability to barter influence for six- and seven-figure political donations, would be neutered. Davis would have to stand on his political record.

A few weeks later, another bombshell: It was reported in a newspaper story that Leon Panetta and Dianne Feinstein had struck a political deal. If she ran for governor, he would not oppose her; and if she won, she would, as governor, appoint him to her vacant Senate seat. While Feinstein's office denied knowledge of any deal, Panetta, it was further reported, smiled enigmatically and said that anything could happen in the future.

As a negotiator, I concluded two things. First, Leon Panetta would not be running for governor of California. If he didn't start now, he could never raise the money to run. Second, Dianne Feinstein had not recovered from her bruising 1994 Senate reelection race against Michael Huffington. She was scared of competition. I couldn't beat her, but I just might be able to bluff her out of the race.

By August 1996 it was no secret that I would be exploring a new chapter in my career. I then chanced to attend a fund-raising luncheon for President Clinton at the home of Dick Blum, my Northwest partner, and his wife, Senator Dianne Feinstein. Each table had two empty places so that the president and senator could circulate among the guests. When President Clinton sat next to me, Dick appeared over our shoulders and said, "Mr. President, don't you think Al would make a great Senate candidate—in Minnesota?" I merely smiled.

In early December, I arranged to have a private dinner with Blum in Los Angeles. I felt that as a professional and personal courtesy, I should tell him what I was contemplating. Besides, having read the newspaper articles about Feinstein and Panetta's deal, this seemed as good a time as any to start the negotiation.

I began by inquiring about Dianne's political plans. He coyly allowed as how she was happy in the Senate and he didn't think she wanted to run for governor. I took the opportunity then to say that I had given a lot of thought to my next steps and decided that I wanted to explore a run for governor myself. He was momentarily speechless. He then counseled me "as a friend" that this was a bad idea, that I didn't know politics, and that I wouldn't have a chance of winning. I told him why I wanted to run and revealed that I intended to fund the race myself to stay independent of special interests. It was clear I'd done a lot of preparation.

He became quite agitated and said, "What if the 800-pound gorilla enters the race?" I took it that he was referring to his wife and barely suppressed a smile. I said that she would indeed be formidable and would probably win, but that I had something to say and wanted to see if it had resonance. I reminded him that I was not afraid to try something and fail.

I asked that, other than advising Dianne, he keep our conversation confidential, as I was still thinking and did not want to go public with this yet. He assured me that he would. As he departed to return to San

Francisco, he looked at me, shook his head, and said, "Well, you never cease to amaze." The game was on.

The next day, I received a call from a friend in San Francisco. "I hear you're running for governor of California." Blum had declared my candidacy! My hand was forced, so I arranged an interview with the *Los Angeles Times* and publicly dipped my toe in the water.

In my first political speech on February 4, 1997, at the Town Hall Forum in Los Angeles, I announced that I would explore a candidacy by traveling the state and seeing if the public was receptive:

> We used to pull together, but now we've lost our sense of inter-connectedness and we seem to have lost our most precious possession: our optimism.
>
> Instead of emphasizing our mutual dependence, we are pitting one group against another, as if communal life was a zero-sum game. Incredible, because as society becomes more technologically advanced, we become more mutually dependent.
>
> Most of our institutions have adjusted to change, but not government. We have lost our commitment to support it. Young people no longer aspire to serve, and few among our successful private citizens consider doing a term of public service anymore.
>
> This wouldn't be so bad except that, contrary to what many would have us believe, government is important. It protects our constitutional rights and performs necessary functions that the private sector cannot. And, most importantly, it does the important work of binding us together.
>
> If we can attract the right people and give them the right direction, we can transform government. This is where leadership can have its greatest effect.
>
> In defining government's new role, we should also seek a public sector that is focused and concentrates where it can be most effective, stimulating and working with the private sector to create jobs and opportunity.
>
> If the only thing state government succeeded in doing was

to help produce full employment at a living wage, we could transform our quality of life. All of our social problems, including crime, would be materially reduced.

A strong society encourages the energies of all its citizens. A fair society not only tolerates but proudly asserts individual rights and opportunity. We must be both strong and fair.

We have in effect developed two standards: more justice and influence for those who have money and power, and less for those who don't. We can't renew confidence in our state and our public institutions if access to government continues to be bought and sold on the auction block of special-interest politics.

I have seen what individuals can achieve when they have leadership and hope and a sense of shared interest. If I enter this race, I intend to win based on the quality of my ideas and the confidence of people in my capacity and commitment to carry them out.

I intend to ask my fellow citizens to support not just a candidacy, but a cause. It is the cause of self-government at its best: the demand for a new politics of hope and positive change; an end to the use of wedges to divide us; and a call to all our citizens to come together and meet their broad civic responsibilities.

The California political press pretty much ignored the substance of what I said and instead focused on my decision to self-fund my campaign. They immediately compared me with Michael Huffington, who two years earlier had contested a Senate seat in a narrow loss to Dianne Feinstein. That Huffington and I had little else in common did not seem to matter.

I proceeded to introduce myself to the people of California by speaking publicly, traveling the state, and meeting with various civic groups. I formed personal relationships with a network of politicians, community leaders, and civically active individuals. I learned a lot and confirmed in my own mind that I really wanted to do the job and serve as California's governor. I could do without the ceremonial aspects; but I loved sitting down with people, mediating between competing interests, and working out ways to solve problems. There were lots of problems to solve; they were challenging; and they mattered.

As I traveled the state, I periodically read in the papers negative comments about myself, principally from Gary South, Gray Davis's campaign manager. He was a master of the outrageous quote. I didn't complain. Gray was a candidate. This was part of the game and South was doing his job. I just wished he wasn't so good at it.

The same didn't hold true, however, for remarks emanating from Dianne Feinstein and her political team of Bill Carrick and Kam Kawata. She was not an announced candidate, so I felt their comments were gratuitous. I wanted her to know that I wasn't going to back down. Whenever the Feinstein camp took a verbal shot, I volleyed one back. Blum called me, apoplectic, and said, "We can't have this." I said, "Dick, you know me. If you throw a punch at me, I'll hit you over the head with an axe. I won't say anything about Dianne if she and her people don't say things about me." Things would be quiet for a while, then they would break the truce. I would give her another verbal love tap and get another call from Blum.

On September 23, 1997, after traveling the state for nearly eight months, I formally declared my candidacy for governor in a speech in Sacramento:

> Starting today, I am a candidate for Governor of California. I believe we need both real-world experience and new ideas that will break fresh ground, challenge special interests, and truly prepare California for the twenty-first century.
>
> In the course of this campaign, I will outline detailed proposals that will put our schools first and make this state first again in education; that will build a prosperity and a society that includes all our people; that will make government an instrument of progress, not political and bureaucratic self-preservation; and that will strengthen the rule of law and our sense of community, so we can secure once again one of the

most fundamental of all civil rights—the right to be safe in our own homes and neighborhoods.

Some insiders say I shouldn't run, and can't win, because I come from outside the political establishment. They say I'll make rookie mistakes. I'm sure I will. But my experience outside politics is precisely why I am running and why I'm convinced we can and must succeed, not only in this campaign, but in changing California in the years to come.

I've spent my life solving problems by working with working people, by recruiting the best talent, and then trusting the power of individual initiative and creativity. You don't have to be a politician to succeed in government. And the truth is that for too long, politicians leading our government have failed.

They can't solve problems when they're spending most of their energy spinning reporters and seeking to turn their opponents' molehills into mountains. They can't raise our sights or raise new ideas when they're devoting most of their time to raising money.

Does anyone honestly believe that elevating another one of them to the governorship will change anything except the name on the door? Every candidate talks about leadership. But what kind of leadership have they given us? It is a leadership that sacrifices the long-term interests of California to a short-term personal interest in national office.

I reject the conventional politics that evades hard choices, that obscures controversial issues and seeks to offend no one except the powerless and the marginal.

My positions aren't cut to fit any ideological pattern; the test for me is simple: what will meet the needs of California and move it forward, not what will satisfy the political establishment or big campaign contributors.

I pledge today to take on the old politics, to stand up for change, to make the hard choices, and to speak for the California we should be. The California we can become.

In late November 1997, I decided to apply a little gas to my candidacy by going up on television with some advertising. Despite traveling the state for nearly a year, there had been very little substantive coverage of my candidacy in the press; I barely registered in public opinion polls. With the February 4, 1998, filing deadline for California state candidates rapidly approaching, I thought it important to show some momentum to discourage the entry of other candidates. Shortly after the spots started airing, as my recognition started to rise in the polls, I got another call from Blum. This one was to "confirm our understanding that if Dianne entered the race, I wouldn't campaign against her." I had always found Blum to be a pretty good guy but not much of a negotiator. I had to laugh at this tactic, though. I explained to Blum that the Hitler-Stalin pact lasted only until Germany invaded Russia.

I had no intention of comparing myself with Dianne if she was not a candidate, but if she declared, we would conduct a normal race. Besides, she couldn't seem to restrain her people from attacking me when she wasn't a candidate. Was I supposed to just grin and bear it if she declared? Blum exploded at my answer, but it wasn't very convincing; he obviously knew better. I don't know if he had told Dianne that he could control me or what was going on, but this had gotten ridiculous. If she wanted to run, she was obviously free to do so. If she wanted a coronation, she could find someone else to be her footman.

I heard from Blum one more time a few weeks before the February filing deadline. Four separate people with whom we were mutually acquainted placed four separate phone calls to me within a period of eight hours. Each had the same message—Dick Blum says that you have three choices: First, drop out of the race and declare your candidacy for lieutenant governor, and Dianne will support you and help you. Second, sign a contract that says if Dianne runs, you will not attack her or do any negative campaigning about her. Third, if you do not choose one of the first two, they will find another candidate, put all of their resources behind them, and run an "Anybody But Checchi" campaign.

"Too bad," I quipped, "they've already dealt away the Senate seat!" I knew that the American political class was lame, but this was really too much. My lawyer and friend, Bert Fields, one of America's top litigators, put in a call to Blum to explain that a) such a proposal would be against the law, b) I was not inclined to consider it, and c) I had no intention of responding to him. According to Fields, when he mentioned the legality of his approach, Blum stammered, "It's not a 'proposal,' but if it is, I retract it."

Shortly thereafter, on January 21, 1998, the *Los Angeles Times* reported:

> In an understated announcement that belied the long buildup, Dianne Feinstein said she had no desire to give up her "creative" work in the Senate for the "conflicted environment" of a campaign—and a race that would have been her third statewide run in five years.

I could only think of my old antagonist T. S. Eliot: "This is the way the world ends: not with a bang but a whimper."

I had won. Dianne Feinstein would not be running for governor of California. But the victory proved Pyrrhic for me, and ultimately for the people of California.

On February 4, a few hours before the expiration of the filing deadline, in a telephone conference call from Washington, DC, Congresswoman Jane Harman announced her candidacy for governor of California. Her campaign, she said, would be managed by Senator Dianne Feinstein's political team, Bill Carrick and Kam Kawata. She further announced that she would take no questions. It appeared that Blum and Feinstein had implemented choice number three: Anybody But Checchi.

It was rumored that the Feinstein team had approached others, including the faithful and patient Panetta, but it was too late for them. Harman, on the other hand, was ready to go. Not particularly popular with her House colleagues, she appeared unlikely to have a future in the House leadership. However, her husband, Sydney, was a billionaire and could easily underwrite her gubernatorial campaign, as he had her initial run for Congress. Although Harman represented a California congressional district, it was only one of fifty-two in the state. She had not lived in California for nearly thirty years, had not traveled the state, and appeared not done any preparation for a gubernatorial campaign.

A few weeks later, she addressed the same Los Angeles Town Hall Forum in which I had announced my initial exploratory effort. Again she announced that she would take no questions, although she did make one memorable statement. Perhaps hoping to woo non-Democratic support in the open primary, she proclaimed herself "the best Republican in the Democratic Party." Two months later, on April 17, the *Los Angeles Times* reported on another Harman appearance: "She said she was not ready to offer specifics on how to solve the state's problems . . . that she never will—at least not before the election." By the time she finally started traveling around the state and began to entertain questions and attempt to speak to the issues, she had been too damaged by the perception that she was unprepared, and her candidacy collapsed.

At first, I thought that Harman understood her assigned role, because her campaign followed such a predictable course. Carrick and Kawata continued to work the press and attack me personally. I had served notice publicly months before Harman entered the race that I would run a positive campaign, but if attacked I would respond directly with paid advertising. I proceeded to point out her voting record in the House and made hay over her line about being such a great Republican (the kiss of death among Democratic primary voters). Her team then returned a barrage of paid media accusing me of running a negative campaign!

As Harman repeatedly proclaimed that she was "running a positive campaign," I came to realize that she was unaware of what kind of campaign she was running or its true purpose. It seemed to me that she wasn't supposed to win—just stop me. The Harmans spent over $16 million during the four months that she was a candidate for governor; little of it appeared aimed to boost her candidacy.

Meanwhile, the principal beneficiary of that candidacy and Sydney's spending was Gray Davis. As Harman collapsed in the polls, her team targeted me with more media. Not only was Davis spared this negative media attention, he experienced a financial windfall from the

Feinstein team's efforts to nullify the recently passed campaign finance reforms.

Bill Carrick, Feinstein's longtime campaign strategist, was one of the principal advocates for overturning the new campaign finance limitations. Commenting for a court hearing in mid-October 1997, Carrick said that placing limits on contributions would be "unfair to traditional candidates like Gray Davis." The courts nullified the people's will and changed the rules in the middle of the race. All contribution limits were overturned and California politicians were again free to raise unlimited amounts from individual contributors.

Davis was back in business. With contribution limits eliminated, he was able to tap the full range of the California "pay for play" spectrum of special-interest money, cumulatively over his career pulling in contributions totaling nearly $3 million from just one public employee union alone, the 26,000-member prison guards. To put this in perspective, this was equivalent on a per-capita basis of receiving campaign contributions of $1.8 billion from the AFL-CIO. Davis applied his media dollars where they would have their greatest effect: against me. In a twist of irony, the career politician who had never actually run anything in his life would use to good effect the tag line "Experience that money can't buy!"

In retrospect, numbers spoke to Gray Davis, too, and he knew how to speak back. Davis, with active support of the public-sector unions, went on handily to win the primary and the general election. One of his first acts as governor was to grant the California prison guards an extraordinary pay increase worth over $500 million per year—in financial terms, a "present value" of over $5 billion on their $3-million investment in Davis's political career, and much better than the Basses had done with Walt Disney!

California's other public-service unions were not forgotten. They received an unprecedented retroactive pension increase that ultimately drove California's total unfunded statewide pension obligations to an estimated $500 billion. And once in office, again true to form, Davis devoted himself relentlessly to raising campaign cash—over $78 million for his next election.

I had funded my own campaign and refused all outside contributions. I thought that this would be deemed positive. One high state union official set me straight. "Everyone knows you would make a better governor than Gray," he said, "but we own him and we'll never own you." He might as well have said, "Welcome to the NFL."

At the risk of sounding like sour grapes, I can safely say that he was right. I would have made a better governor than Gray Davis—but so would have Jane Harman, Leon Panetta, Dianne Feinstein, Dick Blum, and virtually everyone that I know, inside or outside of politics.

Four and a half years later, Gray Davis was *recalled* from the office of governor. It was only the second recall of a governor in American history. Often referred to in print as "the hapless Gray Davis," he mired California in a costly and unnecessary energy crisis, among other missteps. Democratic strategist and pollster Pat Caddell said of him, "Gray Davis was the most incompetent and corrupt governor in California history; we could stand one of them but not both."

As predicted, California continued its precipitous decline. Today it is insolvent. No remotely possible set of conditions exist under which it can meet its long-term financial obligations. It has been running annual operating deficits of $20 billion for years, while there is an estimated additional $15- to $20-billion annual shortfall of deferred infrastructure investment. Taxes are already among the highest in the country, which has caused a net emigration of high-income earners; there is, therefore, little likelihood that raising taxes further could materially increase revenues.

In national surveys, California is listed as the least attractive of the fifty states for business due to its regulatory regime and tax structure. It has lost its banking and aerospace industries, much of its manufacturing base, and many major corporate headquarters. Looming over all is the $500 billion of unfunded benefit obligations contractually promised to public employees.

At this point, it doesn't much matter who is elected to any position in California government, let alone governor. There is nothing anyone can do to close the deficit, pay for vital infrastructure investment, and meet the pension obligations. The political class has killed the golden goose.

Until and unless California goes through some judicial restructuring similar to a corporate bankruptcy, whereby it trims its long-term obligations, reduces public-service compensation to competitive levels, restricts government to its essential functions, and overhauls its regulatory regime to stimulate economic development, California will continue to plumb new depths of civic deterioration.

California governor campaign, 1998.

FIFTEEN

Requiem for a Campaign

"The time has come," the walrus said,
"To talk of many things:
Of shoes—and ships—and sealing-wax—
Of cabbages—and kings—
And why the sea is boiling hot—
And whether pigs have wings."

Lewis Carroll

THE LESSONS I LEARNED on the California campaign trail have nation-wide relevance.

First, since I did not have to raise campaign contributions, I was able to go places and meet people that candidates normally have neither the interest nor the luxury to see. I was personally overwhelmed by the amount of volunteerism I encountered. We are a remarkably generous and compassionate people, regardless of political stripe. So many organizations involving so many people are on the front lines, addressing the needs of their fellow citizens. It is unfortunate so much of their effort must be devoted to fund-raising. Government should explore ways of reducing its inefficient bureaucracies and instead direct its resources through those civic organizations that do so much good with so little.

Second, the corrupt bargains struck between self-interested political careerists and the public-service unions are the primary cause of the fiscal problems of California and of most of the country's states and municipalities. In this regard, I do not blame the union leaders. Their job is to get as much as they can for their members by way of salary, benefits, and job security. They have done a great job—perhaps too great.

The failure, an abject one, lies with the politicians who have bartered away the public's interest in exchange for the political and financial support of the unions. There is no justification for awarding "public servants" greater salaries and benefits than their private-sector counterparts, since they are immune from competition and therefore enjoy largely unlimited job security. In an honest system, public-sector jobs, given their security, would earn a discount to private-sector ones (albeit not as great a discount as the one that forced my father to leave public service).

That salaries and benefits in the public sector average double the annual $62,000 of the private sector is de facto evidence of the depravity of the elected politicians who set these compensation levels. What would the budget of California and every state and municipality in the Union look like if the average amount of total compensation paid to public-sector workers matched the private sector and was therefore reduced by approximately half? How many more services could be provided the public with the savings? How much more infrastructure could be built? How much could individual and corporate taxes be reduced and income returned for investment to expand private-sector jobs?

Third, the role of the press is critical for the public to make informed decisions about the philosophy, integrity, and competence of candidates for public office, as well as their performance once elected. I lost the election fair and square. I have no complaints about the press coverage or the actions (reported and unreported) of my opponents. I would, however, make the following observations.

My campaign was certainly not underfunded. I spent over $38 million trying to get a message to the public: $32 million solely on my own message; $5 million of so-called "comparative advertising," contrasting myself with my opponents; and $1 million directed solely at opponents. Despite the large amount of spending dedicated solely to promoting myself, very few people are aware that I ever ran for public office; fewer are aware that I ran as a Democrat; and almost no one is aware of what I had to say. The public is highly dependent upon the media for education about the candidates as well as the issues. Paid exposure (thirty- and sixty-second television spots) is no substitute for in-depth third-party reporting and analysis. In an article published a month before the primary vote, on May 6, 1998, the *New York Times* noted how little news coverage was accorded the governor race in California:

> In a primary election on June 2, the nation's most populous state will begin choosing a new leader for the world's seventh-largest economy. But except for the millions of dollars in paid advertising that floods the airwaves day and night, hardly anyone would know it. The campaign is all but invisible on television news and only sporadically gets front-page newspaper coverage.

Most of the media coverage of the California race, and in fact much of the media coverage of all political races, local and national, tended to be superficial, dealing with campaign tactics and the horse race. There was precious little attempt to put the contest into context or explain what was at stake for the state and how the various candidates might specifically meet the particular needs of the time.

Speaking solely for myself, the only times that I felt that the situation facing the state and the dimensions of my candidacy were remotely explored were during the one- to two-hour newspaper editorial board interviews that preceded their issuance of endorsements. While I received more endorsements than all of my opponents combined, these editorials were short, one-day articles, seen only by a relatively small audience, quite late in the campaign. *The Sacramento Bee*, considered the paper of record for California state government, published its endorsement on May 17, 1998, just three weeks before the election.

Beneath the sunny skies of a resurgent economy, California remains a state paddling hard against tides of deterioration. Its once-admired public schools are physically rotten and academically inadequate. The economy grows, but still local governments struggle to put enough police on the streets or enough caseworkers on the job to protect children. Our freeways, once a model for the world, are always crowded and often crumbling. The great public university system faces a coming enrollment surge without sure plans or certain funding. State politics are divisive and governance hogtied by a cycle of public cynicism and restrictive initiatives.

"Business as usual" is a recipe for continued deterioration in the Golden State these days; the status quo is no friend. Such circumstances demand bold remedies.

Businessman Al Checchi is the most promising candidate by far. California needs his demonstrated capacity for strategic thinking and willingness to make systematic change. Indeed, his strongest credential is perhaps the simplest to understand: "I change things," he says, and the record backs him up . . .

Can Checchi work cooperatively with other elected leaders in the shared enterprise of governance? His record while building and leading successful teams at Marriott, Disney and Northwest suggests he can. While there is an undeniable element of risk in choosing a governor who has no elective background, there is also a great downside to selecting more of the same, perhaps tilted a little differently.

When the four candidates for governor were asked how to handle the budget surplus expected this year, only Checchi resisted the typical political "loaves and fishes" reply of promising a little something for every program with enough left over for a tax cut. Said Checchi: "So you want to talk about what to do with the surplus? Invest it in the future. . . . That's what we should be talking about, not a car tax."

Those are bold words in California's fractured world of interest-group politics, but they are the right ones. They provide a sharp alternative to the views of Lungren, who will and should be the Republican nominee in the fall. And they offer a clear contrast to Davis, who presents himself as the familiar candidate of the status quo, and Harman, too often positioned as someone who can split the difference with Republicans.

This was clearly a good piece for me. My opponents received endorsements favorable to them. But none of us received sustained coverage aimed at the substance of our qualifications, vision, or programs. Voters need this information.

Further, I believe that too many reporters have become advocates for specific candidates and parties rather than honest brokers. When they do venture beyond horse-race stories, they often present views of the candidates that are highly distorted. The comedian Fred Allen once said, "To a newspaperman a human being is an item with the skin wrapped around it." Some voters are influenced by the bias, but I would argue that most see through it. This is small consolation, though, as this still leaves them without a reliable means of getting an objective view of the candidates.

Fourth, there is no reason for politics to be so partisan. Along the campaign trail, I encountered many who remembered a time when our politics were different. Our leaders had a greater sense of national purpose, and the press assumed a solemn responsibility to keep us informed and the politicians honest. An elderly woman in Santa Barbara spoke for many when she said to me, "I want to believe again, one more time before I die, I want to believe." There is a genuine hunger among people to join again in the shared adventure of participatory democracy. But they crave leadership that brings people together and calls upon the best in us.

Fifth, and finally, when you get to the places where politicians usually don't go and the klieg lights don't shine, there are a lot of people out there who need help, particularly the children, society's innocents. One memory still haunts me: I visited an elementary school in rural Southern California. Most of the children were Latino. I asked the principle how they did. She said, "They do very well until the end of the month. That's when the money runs out and they don't eat." My eyes welled with tears when I recalled the plight of these children during my concession speech, as they often do whenever I tell this story. It is inconceivable to me that a society as rich as ours can allow its children to go hungry.

In the first chapter, I referred to the little girl in Salinas who asked me, at the end of my campaign, if I had ever worked in the fields.

But there was one last question at that club as I prepared to leave.

"Will you forget us?"

I haven't, and I won't.

SIXTEEN
Lost

I wake to sleep, and take my waking slow.
I feel my fate in what I cannot fear.
I learn by going where I have to go.

Theodore Roethke

AFTER LOSING THE 1984 presidential election in a landslide, Vice President Walter Mondale asked Senator George McGovern, who had lost a presidential election by a similar margin a dozen years earlier, "When does the pain stop?" McGovern replied, "I don't know. I'll tell you when I find out."

When I woke up on June 3, 1998, the morning after the primary, with a huge electoral hangover, I knew that things were going to change once again, but for the first time in my life, I had no place to go.

I was not so much in pain as I was numb. After a lifetime of preparation, I had gone all-out for two years in direct pursuit of my dream. In athletic terms, I had left it all on the field. I was fifty years old; the game was over, and the dream gone. My future seemed a blank.

Further, I soon learned that in my absence, Northwest management had missed a step in the ritualized dance of contract negotiations with organized labor and terminated negotiations one round too early, leaving the pilots, in their mind, no choice but to strike. My concentrated holdings of Northwest stock immediately plummeted in value by over $500 million. I hadn't thought much about money up to that point, but this caught my attention. Now I hurt.

If there is any question, losing an election leads to—nothing. I received a few condolence calls, several even from labor leaders saying that they would back me "next time" and a comforting one from President Clinton who said that most everybody loses their first race (as he had), that I had impressed a lot of people, and was well positioned for "next time."

People speak of a Chinese proverb: "Fool me once, shame on you; fool me twice, shame on me." For me, there would be no next time. While I had learned about the process of mounting a campaign and was better on the stump toward the end than I was at the beginning, I had no interest in triangulating or altering my positions to attract the support of special-interest groups in order to win an election. What is the good of winning if you can't make a difference, and how would you do that if you won on false pretenses and had no mandate? I wanted to make big changes, which would require that people understood clearly what I wanted to do and actively supported it.

I took comfort in the fact that I had said my piece and the people chose differently. Winston Churchill declared that democracy was the worst form of government except all the others. In the Charles Schulz comic strip *Peanuts*, the character Linus said, "I love mankind; it's people I can't stand." Despite my less-than-stellar electoral results, I found myself less jaundiced than the prime minister or my comic-strip hero. I love democracy, and I developed a genuine affection and regard for the people that I came to know as I crisscrossed our largest state. I have traveled a good part of the world; there is simply no place like America. And as one of the largest and most diverse of our states, California afforded me a two-year opportunity to appreciate the full grandeur of our country.

As for my feelings about the experience of being a political candidate, I guess you could say that it was something that I felt I had to do—and I gave it my all. Things don't always turn out for the best. And as the song says, "You can't always get what you want."

We would have to change places once again.

SEVENTEEN
New Beginnings

The ultimate result of shielding men from the effects of folly is
to fill the world with fools.

Herbert Spencer

NEARLY ALL GREAT LEADERS have had their periods in the wilderness.
I wasn't sure what I was, but I had the wilderness part down pat. I
resumed my interest in reading, mostly American biography and history.
I took the opportunity to spend more time with my family, reconnected
with friends, and traveled. I revisited the Middle East, South America,
Australia, New Zealand, Scandinavia, and Western Europe. And I did a
lot of thinking and writing.

I also explored new interests. On a dare (I didn't think I could do it),
I took up classical piano and ended up as the understudy for a one-man
show on Broadway—sort of. My teacher, the concert pianist, composer,
and conductor Hershey Felder, had written a one-man play, *George
Gershwin Alone*, in which he would act, sing, and perform Gershwin's
music, including the notoriously difficult "Rhapsody in Blue." Joking
that no other performer could play the role and he would need an understudy, I offered my services. On a lark, he listed me in the Broadway
playbill, with biographical details such as my experience "singing in the

shower." Several Wall Street playgoers actually took this seriously and left their business cards, asking to be notified when I would perform. They're still waiting.

I next set out to master golf. Like many men, I have always felt that if I only had the time to play, I could be good at this game. I proceeded to devote a great deal of time, energy, and money to it. When I subsequently took my game on the road to Scotland and stopped to play a small-town course, I was paired with a twelve-year-old boy. After we had played about six holes, he politely inquired, "Sir, why do you have such expensive golf clubs if you are such a terrible golfer?" Undeterred, I have been hard at it ever since, but have destroyed another of life's illusions. I'll never be any good at this game.

Having satisfied myself that I wasn't going to make it on the concert or golf circuit, I thought about resuming my business career, but my heart just wasn't in it. Business had always been a means to an end for me. Once I had immersed myself trying to figure out the solutions for the problems of a place like California, I just couldn't get excited about the issues facing a single business.

Besides, business, like politics, had changed. Apparently there was now a new paradigm. Neither profits nor cash flow mattered in this "new economy." This was the dot-com era. It was not uncommon for start-up companies with $1 million in annual revenues to receive public market valuations of $1 billion or more, regardless of the fact that they were hemorrhaging cash. All that mattered was what "space" they were in. I wondered what planet everyone was on.

Companies like Global Crossing, aided and abetted by the financial community, would reach stratospheric market valuations based on sales and (ultimately) profit expectations that were pure fantasy. In the great Dot-Com Bubble, unsophisticated investors (which I have learned includes practically everyone) saw the NASDAQ stock exchange crash nearly 80 percent, from approximately 5,050 to 1,100, in a year. Many people lost their life's savings in one of history's greatest orgies of self-delusion.

The private equity industry, based in part on the success of investors like the Bass family, had grown into a colossus. The problem was that it was no longer private. The world had changed a lot since supplicants would come down to Fort Worth to see us at Bass Brothers because we were only one of a handful of places they could go, or when someone like me could casually make a list of twenty public companies that essentially could be bought with their own cash. Those days were over.

Asset valuations had increased over ten times from the mid-1980s to the end of the 1990s. Any investment that was leveraged during these years would have generated high returns. As a result, cash poured into private equity, and there were now countless funds of $1 billion or more, and several of more than $10 billion.

Instead of small private opportunities with little or no competition, nearly 70 percent of the new investments were acquisitions of public companies bought at auction. Many fund managers collected huge sums, essentially for doing little more than bidding against each other. The winner would be the fund willing to pay the most using other people's money. The losers could content themselves collecting large fees on their clients' committed funds until they, too, won at auction and would have a chance to collect an additional 20 percent of any future profits. This was like the song particularly popular in Texas, "Money for Nothing and Chicks for Free." I thought the philosophy behind this was best expressed by Charles Schulz's character Snoopy, "Anything that falls on the floor is legally mine." Win or lose, with minor exception no value was being created. The "masters of the universe" who staffed the private equity firms were not unlike their counterparts in politics. They had never developed the skills to actually add value, only to promote themselves.

There had been a sign posted in the Bass Brothers trading room: "Don't confuse brains with a bull market." For the most part, the historic returns from private equity were merely the result of applying leverage in a bull market. Once the stock market became fully valued, the underlying forces driving leveraged market returns dissipated. Private equity returns from marginal funds collapsed into large losses after 2005. As their commitments to these funds lapse, more pension managers will think twice before letting a cadre of young people experienced only at operating Excel software leverage their investments to play what has largely become a private poker game.

Thanks to the bull market, the money management industry in the United States also grew exponentially over the past twenty years. This too is one of the great triumphs of consumer marketing. While the practices of this industry would shame P. T. Barnum, just as with private equity, there will be a day of reckoning. Abraham Lincoln said, "You can fool some of the people all of the time, and all of the people some of the time, but you cannot fool all of the people all of the time." I think you can pretty well count on the air seeping out of yet another bubble.

There are approximately 135,000 public-equity and debt issues worldwide. Their market prices, posted electronically, result from the twenty-four-hour-a-day actions of millions of investors placing bets about future interest rates, inflation, country risk, industry prospects, technological change, shifts in consumer tastes, fashion, etc. For every buyer who wants a security at a given price, there is a seller who wants to get rid of it. They meet electronically and seamlessly.

All securities have different risk profiles. A comparatively safe short-term US government bond may yield 2 percent, while an airline bond may be priced to produce 10 percent. Through the market, investors are establishing a consensus about their relative risks. The same thing happens in assessing common stocks. They, too, have different expected returns based on presumed risks. The public markets thereby price all securities relative to each other, such that each has a fifty-fifty chance of outperforming its risk-adjusted expected returns.

An entire industry has arisen around the proposition that there are people (tens of thousands, if you can believe their claims) who individually know more than the market (meaning the rest of the world). They presume to predict the future for all the variables that go into the relative pricing of securities and actually pick the winners.

As the late comedian Jimmy Durante said, "Everybody wants to get into the act." Not only are there people who purport to pick the winners (for a fee and then some), there are people who have stepped in to pick the people who pick the winners (for a fee and many sums). Investment bankers and wealth managers of large commercial banks, trust companies, and big-name financial institutions will, for a fee, choose individual money managers for their clients. These chosen managers, they assure, are "top 10-percent" performers. Performance is generally measured based on how well the manager did over the past three years at beating the market (before fees and expenses). The fact that mathematically fully 12 percent of people will guess right on a coin flip three times in a row (and thereby "beat the market") doesn't seem to factor into their analysis.

The large institutions that pick the pickers for a fee also pick their clients' pockets in many other ways. They hold the securities as custodians for a fee. They are brokers who get paid a fee for trading the securities (often as brokers for the managers that they pick for their clients). They are also underwriters who get paid by corporations and governments to distribute securities that they then sell to their clients, collecting yet another fee. They trade for their own accounts, too—selling to their clients for a fee the securities that they no longer want for themselves. They are also "market makers," meaning that they bid for some securities that may not trade broadly, hold them, and then resell them at a spread over what they paid. That spread is an additional hidden fee. All the fees, trading expenses, and excess taxes incurred by short-term trading cost the average public securities account between 5 and 7 percent annually. It is almost impossible, on a net after fees and expenses basis, for any manager to remotely meet the market's averages over any meaningful period. The game is rigged.

When I began my business career, the leaders of these large institutions saw themselves as fiduciaries operating on behalf of their clients' interests, much as government officials then perceived themselves as serving the public's interest. The lost sense of fiduciary responsibility, the priority placed on self-promotion over acquired skill, and the failure to adapt institutions to changed circumstances have created a national leadership crisis in the private as well as the public sector.

I had tried to address these issues in government by running for governor of California, but I was unpersuasive in the Democratic primary election. As I looked at what had happened to the financial services industry, I recognized an area where our family could take direct steps to produce change.

Spearheaded by my son, Adam, who assembled a sophisticated team, and my wife, Kathy, who provided tax and estate-planning input, we created a computerized trading platform that allows us, at only nominal cost, to measure risk and assemble systematically diversified portfolios of the world's public securities. By taking advantage of advances in technology, we can customize and implement virtually any trading strategy or asset allocation on a tax-efficient and highly secure basis and construct portfolios that maximize quantifiable diversification and thereby minimize risk. In other words, at a fraction of the cost charged by the industry, we can produce a better product for the investor.

Adam and his team are producing the kind of change in the investment business that I helped pioneer at Marriott for financing hotels and ultimately entire companies. They are doing the things that leaders do: recognizing change in the environment and instituting change to adapt to it.

Great leaders have a capacity not only to adapt to change, but to anticipate it, but there are limits to the imagination. We would all soon be confronted by a new and totally unanticipated paradigm.

Clockwise: Kathy, Adam and his family, Kristin,
Kate, and my grandmother Dina.

Eighteen
Let's Roll

There is the national flag. He must be cold indeed, who can look upon its folds rippling in the breeze without pride of country. If in a foreign land, the flag is companionship, and country itself, with all its endearments.

Charles Sumner

IN 2001, I TRAVELED to Italy with my oldest daughter, Kristin. She was about to start her senior year at Stanford. This seemed like a good time to spend together, as for her the rigors of a job search and the demands of the real world would soon intervene. We were well over the Atlantic Ocean on our return flight from Rome, when the captain interrupted over the intercom: "Say a prayer for America. We are diverting our flight and will land in Amsterdam in approximately two hours." It was September 11.

When we landed, I was able to get hold of Kathy on my cell phone. "What is going on?" She explained that two planes had flown into the World Trade Center in New York City and that both towers had collapsed to the ground. I had been to the World Trade Center many times, and as I started to tell Kathy that she was exaggerating, I looked up at the television monitor nearby and saw the replay of the scene that has been seared into the memories of all Americans since that day.

It took nearly a week for us to make our way back home, which afforded me plenty of time to think. This was another game-changer. America was under attack. There would be huge repercussions, socially, economically, and politically.

In retrospect, I do not feel that sufficient credit has been rendered to President George W. Bush or appreciation given for what this attack did to his presidency. During the 2000 presidential campaign, Bush had been criticized for his lack of international experience. He was not particularly well traveled and did not evince great interest in the international arena. He made it clear that his interests were domestic.

Calling himself a "compassionate conservative," George Bush said that he intended to build on his experience forging bipartisan consensus as a successful governor of Texas, and that he had a particular interest in improving public education and solving the undocumented-immigration problem. As president, his first major domestic piece of legislation was the No Child Left Behind Act, which he enacted with the support of the liberal lion of the Senate, Teddy Kennedy. It should not be surprising then, that he was sitting in an elementary school classroom reading to small children when he first got news of the 9/11 attacks.

With the hijacking of the planes, Bush's presidency was effectively hijacked. He was eight months into the job when the United States mainland was attacked for the first time since the War of 1812. The country was traumatized as part of the Pentagon lay smoldering and New York City choked on the dust and smoke of the fallen towers. Despite the size of our military and the power of its arsenal, we were unprepared for this kind of enemy, and no one knew when another attack would be launched, or where, or by whom, or by what means.

Bush's presidency was defined and circumscribed. He had to rally his countrymen, defend against further attack, and develop new strategies and structures both to prevent and prepare for new attacks. All else would be subordinate. There was no precedent upon which to rely. He did the job required to the best of his ability, and he made no excuses or complaints. He "manned up," in the current parlance. I think he deserved better from his countrymen than he received—certainly better than he has gotten from his successor. I believe that, like President Harry Truman, history will be kinder to him than were his contemporaries.

In a real sense, the future for all of us was hijacked on 9/11. This was the end of our national innocence. The false sense of security of living in the world's most powerful country was shattered. There were limits to the protection our power could provide. There were "evil-doers," as Bush accurately but inelegantly phrased it. And with these realizations, each of us has been presented new challenges and opportunities.

When I learned of the last words of the passengers of United Flight 93 as they attempted to retake the hijacked plane—"Let's roll"—I heard this as a call to arms. There had been a street saying in my youth: "If you are not part of the solution, you're part of the problem." If I could not take an active leadership role in public affairs, I could at least try to impart some of what I had learned, make a contribution, and help the country regain its equilibrium.

One place where I could help was the airline industry. The events of 9/11 were very damaging to the United States economy, but nowhere greater than in the airline industry. I was no longer an officer of Northwest Airlines, only a board member; but I pitched in, helping with the general effort to obtain some assistance for the industry from the federal government. It would be a pittance compared with the rapacious effects of a week-long closing of the US air-transportation system, the staggering fall-off in air travel as companies and individuals reduced air travel to a minimum, the massive increase in the cost of airport security, and the attendant unprecedented rise in oil prices related to another, more protracted war in the Middle East.

Industry conditions were even worse post-9/11 than they had been during the first Gulf War, a decade earlier. Every airline in the country was bleeding cash, and every management was seeking to renegotiate their labor costs. Twelve years after the successful 1993 restructuring, few of the original key management participants remained at Northwest. I had little confidence in the prospects of the new team to negotiate successfully with labor. I knew what this process would require. In my opinion, they lacked the necessary experience and skill. Since I was unsupportive of management, I resigned from the Northwest board. I watched from the outside as they tried to gain the necessary labor concessions. Eventually, they admitted defeat, and Northwest Airlines declared Chapter 11 in late 2005. Delta Airlines was also forced to file for bankruptcy on the same day.

It had been evident for years that merger and consolidation were essential to the survival of the US domestic airline industry. I reasoned that bankruptcy, which had been unavoidable, provided opportunity. Government regulators opposed consolidation on general philosophical grounds. To them, it would reduce competition. However, widespread bankruptcies demonstrated even to government bureaucrats that there was a structural problem in the industry that only consolidation could cure. But airlines are so complex, financially and operationally, that merging them is very complicated. On the asset side, there is substantial equipment and facility redundancy. Operationally, as demonstrated by Northwest's previous merger with Republic Airlines, merging employee groups represented by different unions working under different contracts can be a nightmare. I reasoned that bankruptcy provided a unique financial and legal medium to harmonize labor agreements and reduce the capital and operating costs involved in combining such complex entities.

I assembled a group of experienced executives and structured and financed a proposal to merge Delta and Northwest Airlines while both were still in bankruptcy. In this manner, the companies could employ the advantages afforded by court assistance that would be lost once they emerged as independent companies. While this was unorthodox, so was much of what I had done during my business career.

It was easy to demonstrate the economic advantages of merger to both companies' creditors and to explain how they could be enhanced through the bankruptcy process. This was important, because maximizing the value of the assets for the creditors is the fundamental legal responsibility of the management and board of directors of a company in bankruptcy. The plan, as explained, entailed making some management changes, principally bringing in a new chief executive officer to run the combined companies, as was done successfully at Walt Disney.

There will always be people who resist change because it is against their self-interest, but my greatest difficulty has been with the people who may be well-intentioned but simply can't envision doing something different. These are the Luddites that populate our bureaucracies and make them lumbering obstacles to progress and innovation. These constitute the "confederacy of dunces" identified by Jonathan Swift that control many of our large institutions, public and private. They are the reason that entrepreneurs are the principal creators of jobs and innovation in America while large companies and government are laggards.

The managements and boards of both Northwest and Delta Airlines actively resisted our efforts and insisted that their companies would be stronger proceeding through conventional bankruptcies, leaving management in place, and then operating as independent entities. They made court filings to this effect and submitted to the court projections of the value this would create for their creditors. They did not tell the court of our approach. Each company subsequently emerged from bankruptcy as an independent enterprise.

In a matter of days, the public value of each company fell to more than 70 percent below the levels submitted to the courts—to the low levels that our group had forecasted would occur if they tried to operate independently. When oil prices rose, as we had further cautioned was probable, each was threatened with a return to bankruptcy. Both then announced that finding a merger partner would be necessary.

Northwest and Delta subsequently determined that they would merge after all. The final terms were significantly less favorable for both than the ones we had originally proffered. The new chief executive officer of the combined companies was the one that we had originally recommended. However, the company was saddled with nearly $4 billion of excess debt and far higher expenses than our proposal would have provided. Later, Continental and United Airlines, subject to the same identifiable market forces, also consummated a merger. The long-anticipated consolidation of the US airline industry, which we had anticipated twenty years earlier when we first acquired Northwest Airlines, was finally nearing completion.

While the airline industry was, as I had argued before Congress, "the single greatest industrial casualty" of the Gulf Wars and 9/11, the rest of the private sector was also thrown into chaos. Americans are so preoccupied with the future that we tend to ignore the lessons of the past. This is as true today, as we confront high unemployment and a stagnant economy, as it was in early 2003, in the aftermath of the 9/11 attacks.

In March 2003, I spoke before a large business audience in Los Angeles and tried to offer some perspective to the shellshocked assembly. Unsurprisingly, much of what I said followed from my business experiences and mirrored the convictions that I had expressed five years earlier as a political candidate. I would say the same things today:

> In my business career, I have seen 21-percent interest rates, double-digit inflation, oil embargoes and gas lines, political paralysis (an attorney general, a vice president, and a president from the same administration having to resign), and then, courtesy of the last administration, the challenge of explaining the meaning of "oral sex" to my mother-in-law!
>
> I've learned that whatever the circumstances, people assume that they will persist forever. Those of us who raise capital remember the conventional wisdom—in the early 1970s, the Arabs would dominate the world; by the late 1970s, it was the Germans; in the early 1980s, it was the Japanese; and in the late 1990s—some of you are here—American venture capitalists. And as we all remember, in 1780, it was the French!
>
> Whatever the circumstances, people assume they will last forever. In our economy, bubbles will never burst, and downturns will never reverse. But things are always changing, because our society is built on a dynamic fault line—a vigorous private sector and large public sector that are constantly agitating and pressing against each other.
>
> I believe that the health of our system is a function of the health of both our public and private institutions.

I went on to lay out my concerns about what was happening to the balance between the public and private sectors and the deterioration of their leadership. I also cautioned that the public was not going to stand idly by and watch the corporate and political elites divide up society's spoils.

The public and private sectors exist at the sufferance of the people. With respect to our large and robust private sector, there is no constitutional protection for capitalism. The autonomy of business has always fluctuated with the will of the people. Looking back to the 1920s, capitalism was king. We had a laissez faire economy with little regulation, and we had small government. Calvin Coolidge was president, and he could say that "the business of America is business" and not get impeached!

But the 1930s brought widespread financial abuses, bank failures, and the Great Depression that shattered public confidence. When Franklin Roosevelt became president, there were two competing economic models in the world—communism, as practiced by the Soviet Union, and fascism, as practiced by Germany and Italy—but we settled on a third way. We called it democratic capitalism, which is free enterprise with a leash. Under this system, along with preserving free enterprise, we saw the emergence of the SEC, bank regulations, several other new government agencies, higher taxes, and big government.

In a partial reversal, during the past few decades, we've seen a trend toward more economic freedom. We have lower taxes—while we complain about them, not long ago, marginal income tax rates were 70 percent in this country. We permit far greater business and financial consolidations, and we have deregulated many industries.

We had a Democratic president declare the end of big government, and presently the private sector has nearly 70 percent of the economic activity in our country. But what about the future? I must tell you that the recent political and economic trends have disturbing similarities with the 1920s. We have become a much more materialistic society. This is not a moral judgment, just an observation. We have changed.

I then spoke about the dot-com bubble and all the unproductive and risky behavior in the financial markets.

While all this fiddling has been going on, Rome was burning, and real people have been getting singed. The middle class is shrinking. Income disparity has grown to a historic high. We have created parallel existences. We all used to be middle-class, but that's not the case anymore. We now have different schools, different health care, different economic security—arguably different prospects for life, liberty, and the pursuit of happiness.

During this period, there has also been deterioration in our sense of fiduciary responsibility. Employees, customers, companies, whole communities became expendable. We joked about this at the time. There was R.J. Reynolds—the barbarians at the gate. We had Penn Square and that clown drinking beer out of a boot. The annual Drexel conference became popularly known as "The Predators' Ball." But rather than heed the warnings and reform ourselves, things got worse with the bubble economy in the 1990s. In the aftermath, we experienced a major loss of jobs, pensions, and savings for working people. We saw trusted fiduciaries and advisors become predators. Respected names like Enron, Arthur Anderson, and WorldCom grew to live in infamy. It could be truly said that many business people adopted the ethics expressed by George Washington Plunkett of Tammany Hall, who said, "I seen my opportunities, and I took 'em."

I believe that today people especially seek leadership because they are more frightened than I have ever seen. They're frightened about their physical security, and they're frightened about their economic security. I also believe that when the current obsession about war and terrorism abates, people are going to focus more on their economic needs. They're going to demand accountability for the freedom they ceded over to private-sector leadership. They're going to demand answers for lost pensions, lost savings, lost jobs, miserable schools, and they're going to demand change.

Our society has benefited mightily from the present division between the private and public sectors. But we'd all do well to remember the cautionary words of the Emperor Napoleon: "There is but one small step from the sublime to the ridiculous." I believe that we have taken more than a few steps the last several years. And unfortunately, many of those steps were over the line. Now it's necessary for all of us to step forward and justify our leadership roles. We have to clean up and punish abuse. We have to reestablish ethical standards in our organizations. We have to prepare to meet the challenge to participate actively in a coming dialogue that's going to be both vigorous and consequential.

The country was in trouble, not just because terrorism would be a continuing threat or we were in the throes of another economic downturn. Americans had for good reason lost confidence in their institutions. Leaders in both the public and private sectors had abandoned their fiduciary responsibilities. In the private sector, production had given way to plunder, and in the public sector, democracy had been suborned by a cadre of self-perpetuating political careerists.

I felt that the private sector would right itself; markets impose discipline. Sooner or later, the results speak for themselves, as they have in deflating every past bubble and exposing the absurdity of every crackpot "new paradigm." As investors experience the results of taking asymmetrical risks in stable or down markets, they will make the appropriate portfolio adjustments. These might be costly lessons, but not fatal. They might even be good for the soul, as more of the young future business leaders of America learn that there is no free lunch, and you have to create something to get something.

The real problem lay in the public sector. It has no self-correcting market mechanisms. During the past half century, representative democracy has seriously eroded. Americans have come to be governed by an aristocracy—those who control and are employed by the government and, to a lesser extent, those who purchase favor from it. The political parties stand as sentinels guarding the status quo, effectively protecting political orthodoxy from the potential heresy of new ideas. The political establishment may in the short run ignore the need to change and indeed revel in their apparent immunity from the public's will, but they fail to realize the vulnerability of straddling the tectonic forces of an increasingly engaged and enraged public.

As I traveled the country, I saw the low regard with which the political elite were held outside of Washington and the Northeast. I had witnessed firsthand their increased arrogance. The people's perspective was probably best summed up by the joke about the lady who said, "I never vote; it only encourages them."

These political types might be tolerated as long as things were going along fairly well. But things weren't going well. People were scared. And when the financial system finally buckled under the wild speculation and wholesale disregard of risk, the little old ladies, the young, and everyone else voted in large numbers for Hope and Change.

NINETEEN
Hope and Change

We know what a person thinks not when he tells us what he thinks, but by his actions.

Isaac Bashevis Singer

FOR THE FIRST TIME in my life, I volunteered to help a political candidate. I heard the call for change, for bipartisanship and inclusiveness, neither red state nor blue, neither black, white, or brown skin, and I bit— for a while. The young senator from Illinois was saying many of the same things that I had said ten years before.

Very early in the primary process, I was put in contact with Charles Ogletree, the distinguished Harvard Law School professor who had been a mentor to both Barack Obama and his wife, Michelle. Charles sang Obama's praises but pointed out that he had never run anything nor had anyone around him; and nobody in his inner circle had any business experience. Would I help?

I said that I was impressed with his oratorical skills (would that I had them) and his general message, but that I had a lot of detailed questions that I would want to ask him directly. He agreed to set up a meeting. After about three months, Charles was unable to get the attention of the campaign and no meeting ever came about. Having been through a campaign myself, I didn't think too much about it. They didn't know me, and they were probably in chaos.

But my questions were never answered either directly or by the campaign as it unfolded. In fact, as I listened further and learned more about the candidate's background, more questions were raised. In the end, I determined that I could not support or vote for Barack Obama. I explained my reasoning in another unpublished article (this one submitted to the *Los Angeles Times*) that I wrote a few weeks before the general election:

> Seven months ago, in the Democratic primary, based on my belief in his potential, I voted with enthusiasm for Barack Obama. I presumed that he would be required to answer the questions arising from his past associations and actions and explain in detail his vision for the future. Unfortunately, since then, the media has not subjected him to the same critical scrutiny that it routinely applies to other candidates. In this respect, in my estimation, they have done him and us a disservice. He remains, at a time of great uncertainty, unexamined and unexplained—a man with a gaping disconnect between his past and his promise, his words and his deeds.
>
> Every four years, analysts tell us that this is the most important election of our lifetime. Like a broken clock, this time, they might be right. Given a degree of economic turmoil unseen since the Great Depression, responses by government will have serious long-term consequences. In the 1930s, these gave rise to communism, fascism, socialism, and dictatorship in parts of Europe and Asia. In contrast, the United States responded with a series of discrete, pragmatic policy adjustments that preserved and strengthened our unique political and economic system.
>
> At that time, there were also in America many admirers and advocates of fascism, communism, and Russian-style socialism and central planning. Fortunately, based on his personal history and experience, newly elected President Franklin Roosevelt was no ideologue or political extremist. He was imbued with

a positive vision of American exceptionalism. As a member of one of America's most prominent families, cousin of a president, former assistant secretary of the Navy, and governor of New York, he did not see America as a problem. He saw it as a solution. He did not seek to change the American system of self-government and free enterprise; rather, he sought to preserve and protect it.

The recently passed "federal bailout" is not the end of this fiscal crisis, nor is it the beginning of the end, or even the end of the beginning. The next president will make a series of decisions that cumulatively will determine the future shape and nature of our political and economic system. Will he, like Roosevelt, tinker with the specifics but remain committed to our historic way of life? Or will he attempt to impose wholesale another vision based on a different set of values, experiences, and ideology?

Based on what I know of his personal history and experience, I am unwilling to take a chance on Barack Obama. This is as much because of what I don't know as what I do.

What do I know? Barack Obama has had an unprecedented and meteoric rise to the threshold of the American presidency. He built his career on the South Side of Chicago, a fiefdom of the powerful Daly machine. It is doubtful that he or anyone could have risen as he has unless he was a smooth cog in that machine, and there is no evidence that he ever challenged the "Chicago Way." His famous call for the United States not to intervene in Iraq occurred while he was a state senator during an antiwar rally in his liberal district. He first worked in that district as a community organizer for a group modeled upon the principles of the socialist Saul Alinsky. His local congressman was Bobby Rush, the former Black Panther. His pastor was the radical Jeremiah Wright. His earliest political sponsor was his neighbor, William Ayres, the former radical Weatherman. One of his financial patrons was convicted local slumlord Tony

Rezco. Say what you may, this is a far cry from Roosevelt's Hyde Park.

During his brief stay in the US Senate, Senator Obama earned the highest rating by the liberal Americans for Democratic Action. Other than voting with his party, he has left no material footprints in the US Senate, just as he left no notable legacy in the Illinois State Senate, where he appears to have often voted "present" when confronted with politically controversial decisions. As a law lecturer, he wrote no legal articles, and by his own admission in his two autobiographies, his efforts as a community organizer had little material effect. He has already backtracked on promises made for this campaign that he would limit himself to public financing, participate in an extensive series of town hall debates, and engage in a different type of politics (his campaign tactics, while not worse, are certainly not any better than others). Senator Obama has talked about "change" and talked about "bipartisanship" but has yet to actually effect much of either since he left law school.

What I don't know and question: Can a man who has never had to make executive decisions and take responsibility for their consequences and who has never been faced with vetoing extreme legislation proffered by leaders of his own party lead our country through a crisis, preserve our system of democratic capitalism, and free himself from the ideological tethers of the big-city Chicago ultraliberal machine that elevated him?

When queried about his past associations and unprecedented rise through the labyrinth of Chicago politics, as well as their possible effects on his views as a decision maker, Barack Obama dismisses them as irrelevant. Yet his stated positions on unrestricted abortion, green energy, government-mandated and -funded health insurance, elimination of the secret ballot to encourage unionization, restriction of school choice, wealth redistribution, trade, and expansion of government are neither new nor imaginative. They are the standard litany reflecting the worldview espoused by one end of our political spectrum. While they garner near-universal support among Hollywood and urban elites, organized labor, the mainstream media, the more liberal elements of the Democratic Party (like moveon.org), and European social democrats, they hardly seem a plausible basis for the senator's promise of bipartisanship. It is axiomatic: An Obama administration will disappoint either his supporters on the left or those attracted, as I was, by his professed commitment to bipartisan and therefore centrist government.

I believe that our country and our way of life are constantly threatened by extremes, whether on the political left or right. To me, both are equally dangerous, particularly at a time of economic instability. I am concerned that Barack Obama resides on one of those extremes. I hope that I am wrong, as it appears that he will win in November, but under the present circumstances, at this critical time of transition for our country, I cannot advocate taking the chance and supporting him.

I had built a career analyzing circumstances, divining their inevitable results, and designing better ways to meet desired objectives. Unfortunately, I have never been as prescient as I was in my analysis of Barack Obama's experience and fitness to lead our country in these troubled times. I would also say that the deficiencies that I outlined about the press after my gubernatorial race have never had such grave consequences.

Barack Obama, irrespective of his political ideology, is simply one of the least credentialed men ever elected president of the United States. He was a community organizer, a law lecturer, a small-time state legislator, and did a two-year pass through the US Senate.

I venture no opinion on his ideology, only his preparation and ability to do the job. During the two years of his presidency, he has evidenced little understanding of economics or business; neither has he shown knowledge of the most basic principles of management or the fundamentals of leadership, particularly in time of crisis.

In the midst of a collapsing economic recovery and gathering loss of political support, rather than articulate a clear vision and strategy for renewal, he instead proceeded to blame his predecessor for the country's ills while awarding himself, on *The Oprah Winfrey Show*, "a solid B-plus" for his first year's effort.

I can understand the self-satisfaction of a young man who has been awarded the Nobel Peace Prize just for showing up, who has never been knocked about by the likes of Gary Wilson or faced the kind of trial by fire that I endured steering Northwest Airlines to safe harbor amidst war and industry collapse. By stretching his megawatt smile, he had gotten further than anyone in American history. But he gleaned precious little experience and developed no record of relevant achievement for providing substantive value for the country.

Barack Obama ascended to the presidency promising change, but he had never produced or even undertaken to produce it. He surrounded himself with people like him, academics and political careerists, who also had no experience running, let alone changing, large institutions. To my mind, they have gone about the process all wrong. Rather than responding to the environment and creating new structures appropriate to the twenty-first century, they attempted to impose old structures that had been tried and largely discarded in the mid-twentieth century—with little understanding or regard for how they fit the needs of today.

Forcing institutional change top-down—centralizing power, decision-making, and control—runs completely counter to the practices of modern competitive institutions that decentralize decision-making, disperse power and responsibility, and allow those closest to problems to customize their own solutions.

I have seen too many institutions fail because their leaders lacked the vision, imagination, skill, or humility to change with changed circumstances. The Obama administration seems to have arrived with a fixed agenda based on the past at a time when it needed to create something new in anticipation of the future.

The stimulus package is a glaring example of the tremendous cost to the country of electing a man lacking the experience and training to make substantive fiscal decisions.

At a time of great uncertainty, this administration committed nearly $1 trillion of discretionary spending, ostensibly to produce jobs for Americans and "stimulate" the economy. The administration dropped this huge macro-spending amount into a computer model and specifically calculated and announced that jobs would be produced and unemployment held to 8 percent.

Anyone with experience in the real world knows that these models are barely reliable for predicting the direction of events, let alone forecasting a specific result like "8 percent" unemployment. I learned that at Amherst College in a first-year economics course that I barely attended.

More incredibly, this gargantuan amount of resources was turned over to a Congress largely composed of financial illiterates, to spend as its members deemed fit. It doesn't seem to have occurred to them that how the money was spent, not how much, would be the determining factor of how many jobs were created or how much economic growth would result.

If, for example, the entire amount were spent on personnel-intensive projects like Roosevelt's Works Progress Administration (WPA), we probably could have reduced unemployment in America to near zero. We might not get a lot of long-term stimulus, but we would certainly have produced American jobs, and lots of them.

If some of the money had been spent on the personnel-intensive task of constructing a barrier to secure our border with Mexico, we might not only have produced jobs, but we could have eliminated one of the greatest obstacles to developing a consensus as to how to deal with our large undocumented-immigrant population. It should be clear that Americans are not going to agree to any solution embracing our estimated 10 million undocumented residents until and unless they are reasonably satisfied that our borders are sealed—that we are not merely creating an inducement for more illegal migration into our country.

We could have invested the funds strategically—developed a comprehensive program to make America energy independent. We could have created mechanisms to finance greater oil exploration, extraction, and distribution, clean-coal development, and nuclear plant construction. We could have simultaneously harnessed our scientific and engineering capabilities and embarked on a Manhattan-type project to develop alternatives to fossil fuels. Collectively these investments could have made a significant dent in the nearly $1 trillion a year that we transfer to foreign oil-producing interests, many of whom are rogue governments that seek our destruction. This would have stimulated the American economy for generations, while also advancing our national security interests.

Instead of a strategy commissioned by the chief executive and programs designed and implemented by the executive branch of government, the initiative was turned over to Congress. Who in Congress managed this process? Who designed the strategy to target what the benefits would be and made the critical decisions, be they jobs for Americans or long-term investment in America's economic future? Who performed the analysis to see that the programs selected would achieve their targets? Who is managing the implementation of this massive investment of public resources? How has President Obama ultimately managed the largest investment by any government in recorded history?

The results speak for themselves. It appears that in its zeal to "never let a serious crisis go to waste," the administration doled the funds out to 535 legislators and hundreds of government bureaucrats to pursue a deferred wish-list of projects that had been passed over and deemed nonessential or inadvisable for years. Small wonder so many were "shovel-ready," as the money appears to have disappeared down a hole.

Turning to the various bailouts, if an airline that has a far more complicated capital structure, multiple unions, and complex local, state, federal, and international contracts and regulatory relationships could be restructured in bankruptcy, rest assured that restructuring a manufacturing company like General Motors would have been child's play, particularly with the US government acting as a backstop lender of last resort. Instead, the administration intervened on behalf of the United Auto Workers, set aside the legal rights of bond holders, and pumped public funds indiscriminately into the equity of a company that still hasn't addressed the basic structural cost issues, which would have been resolved as a matter of routine in any normal bankruptcy proceeding.

Subsequently we learned that an additional colossal subsidy was buried in the fine print of the enabling legislation. General Motors received an extraordinary unreported $45-billion tax deduction. How many people even knew about this? Did anyone read the contract? Does anyone bother with such details? What public policy did this serve?

The restructuring of AIG was a similar case of waste. Why would the US government pay 100 cents on the dollar to settle AIG's obligations? I would have been happy to reprise my Bass Brothers role and take only one-tenth of 1 percent of the savings that could have been easily negotiated with the AIG creditors, many of which were foreign financial institutions. I don't know that any financial restructuring has missed greater opportunity. I do know that no "serious crisis" has ever created more waste.

Then there is the health-care bill. I simply consider this a crime against democracy for its timing, substance, and the process by which it was enacted.

With financial dislocation deemed so serious as to require a $700-billion infusion to save the banking system, and the American economy on such unchartered ground, what possible legitimate justification could there have been to think that this was the time to restructure one-sixth of the US economy? Clearly, it has been demonstrated that policy makers could not even predict the one-year effect on only one variable (unemployment) when they designed the stimulus package.

Why would anyone think, even in a stable economic environment, that they could predict the behavior of hundreds of institutions and millions of individuals, anticipate their responses to a massive restructuring of such a complex part of our economy, and make remotely accurate forecasts over a period of decades? This to me was the height of irresponsibility and self-delusion.

Substantively, the horse-trading required to cobble together a bare partisan majority in the US House of Representatives and Senate produced a Rube Goldberg contraption involving the establishment of 150 government departments and agencies. Individual lawmakers took it upon themselves to define what coverage insurance companies must provide, who must get it, and who will pay for it (unless of course they refuse). This was all neatly summarized in a 2,000-page instruction book, written in indecipherable language that no one bothered to read. Who managed this process to assure that the parts fit together, that it wouldn't make the quality of health care worse, or that it wouldn't bankrupt the country?

Tellingly, there came a point in the health-care debate when the opposition of the American people was so great that the politicians openly discussed the political (not the economic or practical) merits of dropping the bill. In an act of pure cynicism, they determined that *they* would be better off passing it. As the subsequent midterm elections demonstrated, they couldn't even get that right!

More fundamental to the problems that we face with our leadership, the process by which the health-care legislation was analyzed and presented was intellectually dishonest, if not purposely deceptive. It has left the American people with a program that, unless largely repealed, will be financially ruinous.

The word "lie" is bandied about indiscriminately in our politics. But what can one say?

Many things: The analysis presented to Congress and the American people to justify the costs of this legislation was *inadvertently deceptive*. Or, a cursory examination of the financial and behavioral assumptions only *seems* skewed toward lowering the projected expenses and inflating the benefits. Maybe, the conceit of projecting ten years of revenues and only five years of benefits to produce a projected match between costs and revenues is an *artful analytic technique*. Better yet, to tout a program that adds trillions of dollars to federal spending and describe it as not adding a cent to the federal deficit is merely *poetic license*. I believe that this may be the most irresponsible and self-destructive piece of legislation ever passed in the history of the United States Congress. If it is not repealed and thoroughly redesigned, it will have catastrophic long-term effects on the United States economy and our way of life.

Just as he was awarded the Nobel Prize for peace before he had accomplished anything with respect to war, peace, or anything else, well before he took the oath of office, Barack Obama was favorably compared by the US press with Franklin Roosevelt and Abraham Lincoln.

However, when confronted with an economy in depression with 25-percent unemployment and no mitigating social welfare infrastructure, Franklin Roosevelt rallied a country by saying, "We have nothing to fear but fear itself." By comparison, President Obama faced a recession with only 10 percent unemployment in a country with a highly developed social safety net. Instead of rallying the country and projecting optimism, as did Roosevelt under far more dire circumstances, Obama magnified the country's fear and discontent repeatedly telling the American people that this is the "largest downturn since the Great Depression," and that *he* inherited this "mess." In doing so, he appeared most interested in finding excuses for himself and only succeeded in further undermining public confidence.

A real leader might have said something like:

We have been tested like this before and always emerged stronger than ever. We are blessed with extraordinary resources and the world's most creative and entrepreneurial people. It is at times like this that we are at our best. All we have to do is pull together. We will take care of those who cannot take care of themselves. We will leave no man, woman, or child behind. The rest of us will put our shoulder to the wheel and go about our business with renewed effort and build a strong prosperity for all.

It sure beats "Never let a serious crisis go to waste," as Obama's chief of staff Rahm Emmanuel said shortly after the administration took office.

Abraham Lincoln, with whom Obama was also favorably compared, led the country through its most wrenching period of division, a civil war consuming nearly a million American lives. Yet after four years of horrific war he could say:

With malice toward none, with charity for all . . . let us strive on to finish the work we are in . . . to do all which may achieve and cherish a just and lasting peace among ourselves and with all nations.

In contrast, despite enjoying huge congressional majorities and passing virtually all of his proposed legislation, President Obama repeatedly referred to his political opposition as "enemies" and thereby demonstrated the emptiness of his promise of bipartisan leadership. While Lincoln called on us "to bind up the nation's wounds," Barack Obama spoke somewhat less eloquently about his political opponents "driving the car into a ditch . . . and wanting the keys back."

There have been twelve American presidents during my lifetime. Some were better than others. I am saddened to say that President Obama has done by far the most serious economic damage to this country. At the time that America most needed a leader, he has been found lacking in the experience and depth of character that form the basis for sound judgment and the capacity to deal with adversity.

While I had not voted for him, when Barack Obama won election, I was among the vast majority of Americans who registered their approval and good wishes. I was hopeful and optimistic that perhaps I was wrong and that he was all that he claimed to be, and that despite his limited experience, he might be some kind of savant. He is not. I feel that he has not ameliorated our problems; he has made them worse. I believe that we must look elsewhere for leadership in 2012.

TWENTY
Common Sense

Revolutions are not made; they come. A revolution is as natural
a growth as an oak. It comes out of the past. Its foundations are
laid far back.

Wendell Phillips

A MERICA IS AT A tipping point. While we are still the world's reigning
super power, we are declining. The American people are gravely
concerned about their future. There is a haunting sense, often unexpressed, that, absent intervention, we are the end of a long gray line—the
current generation of middle-aged Americans may be the first to fail to
provide a better life for their children.

There is also a growing sense of disconnect, verging on betrayal,
between the American people and their elected leaders. By large majorities, they have voiced no confidence in the way that Washington does
business.

It should be clear that Americans will not "go gentle into that good
night." We are not prepared to abdicate our position of global leadership,
to surrender our independence, or to forfeit our heritage of exceptionalism. The new paradigm of a political leadership that is self-serving,
self-perpetuating, and devoid of any sense of public purpose has run its

course. The self-anointed aristocracy that has dissipated our inheritance and mortgaged our future must be deposed.

America was forged from unique circumstances. Here the individual is sovereign. As colonists, we waged violent revolution against the perceived tyranny of distant and comparatively minor infringements on our "rights as Englishmen." Independent political activism and, most importantly, the habit of liberty are ingrained in our DNA. In the face of unprecedented economic and civic decline and government dysfunction, our citizens are poised to rekindle the fires of activism that they have historically demonstrated in abundance.

Our representative democracy has seriously eroded. The two major political parties have rendered the fundamental premise of democracy—"government of the people, by the people, and for the people"—a facade. Despite their pretensions, the extreme Orange County Republicans and San Francisco Democrats are codependents serving as financial conduits between a disparate collection of interest groups and a class of political careerists.

It is impossible for visionary leadership to survive the vetting processes of these ideologically rigid political parties as currently constituted. Would any real change agent subordinate his personal principles to collaborate with individuals and interest groups so wedded to avoiding change? Unless coerced, would either of the political parties sponsor such an apostate? If one travels the country and gets away from the Washington/New York echo chamber, one hears that most Americans seek something beyond the Hobson's choice presently offered by them.

To many, Republicans seem to proffer an unregulated society benignly indifferent to the interests of the less fortunate. Solutions to problems are largely limited to cutting taxes, shrinking government, and opposing nearly all public sector endeavors. As currently expressed, Republican orthodoxy fails to provide a positive vision of what government should do. It fails to project an understanding that, as society becomes more complex, our mutual dependence increases. The model of the rugged individual capable of sustaining himself might have once been appropriate for a frontier society with boundless free land and readily available resources, but today mere survival is a social process involving a complex series of relationships. If we ever were, we are no longer islands unto ourselves.

The Democrats, however, counter with an even more extreme vision: a collective welfare state inimical to the requirements for economic growth, where income redistribution, government expansion, and absolution from personal responsibility seem the operative solutions. This is individualism without the individual. It is an economic and social model that has failed every historical test of practicality or desirability. And it runs entirely counter to our history and culture.

When the parties have attempted to create further separation, cross over, and tread in matters of conscience, they have succeeded only in creating unbridgeable fault lines for most Americans. Most of us are fed up with peripheral issues like gay marriage, abortion, stem-cell research, assisted suicide, etc. We may not want to marry someone of the same sex, abort a fetus, contribute our stem cells, or opt for an assisted suicide, but we don't want to prevent anyone else from making their own decisions in these matters, and we don't want government employed as an activist or advocate, either. We want political leadership instead to address the critical overarching issues of a government that has overpromised and underperformed, pursued policies that infringe on individual liberty, exacerbated and perpetuated social divisions, squandered resources, and retarded economic growth.

Each party bases its ideology on a utopian vision. However, in the real world, public and private institutions are powerful and power does indeed corrupt. Individuals are neither perfect nor perfectible. Markets are not necessarily efficient. Cultural differences are profound (and many are unbridgeable). Resources are constrained. Technological progress can be socially regressive. And there are people—many of them—who want to destroy us. Under these circumstances, ideological purity is the default position of the self-deluded and the demagogic. It is no basis for governing. Yet political power in America seems to vacillate between two unworkable extremes.

The consequences of our political dysfunction are not just an unresponsive political system and a dearth of competent, responsible leadership. They are measured in the deterioration in the life of every American, the profligate growth of government spending, the unsustainable accumulation of national debt, and the consequent dimming prospects for our children. They are etched in crumbling bridges and gridlocked highways. They are shuttered in prisons that further crime and drug addiction. They are reflected in the deepening plight of those whose lives are most precarious: the growing numbers of elderly, infirm, and poor. They are registered in the outsourcing of investment and well-paying jobs and the consequent shredding of middle-class opportunity. Ultimately, they are seen in the squandering of a legacy, the dissolution of community, and the forfeiture of a dream.

We are all fortunate to have lived in an era when our country was the unquestioned leader and most powerful nation on Earth. We have truly been the world's indispensable country; all of mankind has shared in our providence. We tipped the scales to free Europe from Nazi domination, to block and roll back Soviet expansion, and to thwart aggression in South Korea and Kuwait. We stand sentinel, protecting humanity from untold numbers of invasions, atrocities, and deaths. The world would be a far different place had we not been willing and able to project our collective values and, when necessary, impose our will to keep the world safe. Our own lives would be far different if this power had been vested in another country.

Although we have been favored by Providence since our conception, we have also struggled and sacrificed to earn and maintain our place in the sun. Our forefathers pledged their "lives and sacred honor" and risked all to secure our liberty and independence. Their grandsons fought a bloody civil war to preserve the Union and secure our Manifest Destiny. Our fathers and grandfathers sought to preserve and bestow the benefits of freedom across the globe and fought two World Wars, a Cold War, and numerous regional conflicts toward this end. Today we are called to face different challenges.

We are not who we were fifty years ago. We are a far less homogeneous people. Our social norms and structures have changed, some radically. Technology has advanced at light speed, giving us vast new capabilities and presenting equally large new challenges. Our economy has changed; markets are now global, presenting unique opportunities and difficulties. Work has changed. Competition has changed. How we learn has changed. Even life expectancy has changed. The world has changed, too. It is smaller, and it is larger. It is stronger and weaker. Our position within it has been inextricably altered.

In my favorite American novel, *Moby Dick*, the narrator, a metaphorical everyman, lists all of the potential meanings heaped upon the great white whale, and asks, "Wonder ye then at the fiery hunt?" Should we have any doubts about what is now at stake for us, our society, and all of mankind? We must develop a new politics and political leadership: to repair and reform our bloated and misdirected government, to contend with the vast changes that have occurred in our society since the New Deal established much of our institutional infrastructure, and to forge entirely new strategies and structures that meet and anticipate the challenges of a twenty-first century remarkably still in its infancy.

I think that most Americans would agree that we need leaders who are qualified and committed as true fiduciaries and who will direct policy to serve the best interests of all and make government again our servant. We want to see the executive and legislative branches function honestly, efficiently, and effectively, giving fair value to taxpayers and equal consideration and representation to all people.

We want to see the government redirect its resources exclusively toward those essential functions that only government can and should perform—those that the private sector can't do, won't do, or we wouldn't trust it to do.

We want to reclaim our government from the legions of political camp followers who feed off the spoils of victory, and instead replace them with people with the requisite character, professional skills, and experience to analyze our complex problems and design and implement pragmatic, nonpartisan solutions.

And we want leaders who can seek and inspire broad participation from citizens not directly employed in formal public service—leaders who will create transparency and renew the shared sense of opportunity, privilege, and responsibility underlying civic participation in a democratic society.

For the first time in history, we have changed party control of Congress during three consecutive presidencies. Those who dismiss the Tea Party movement as artificial as Astroturf, pawns of an unseen Machiavellian force, racists, or fools are simply whistling past the graveyard. These forces have been building for many years. They have finally reached critical mass and achieved broad public expression. They are the spontaneous outcry by an aroused citizenry that is saying "Enough." In this respect, they are no different from the people who, during the 1960s of my youth, registered their disapproval of the status quo and marched to end a war and affirm civil rights.

And if you listen to what they are saying and ignore the occasional wingnut, they certainly aren't radicals. They want the country to return to its founding principles of limited government, maximum freedom, and protection of individual rights. If they were here today, where would our founding fathers Washington, Adams, and Jefferson stand? With the professional politicians who have perfected the art of fund-raising, spinning, and spewing venom, who pass 2,000-page laws without reading them and then question the intelligence of the public for not accepting them, and who consider public office a matter of personal privilege and divine right? Or would they take to the streets with an aroused citizenry marching, however haltingly, to the echo of the patriot's refrain— "We, the people," seeking to rout an entrenched political aristocracy, reestablish limits to the power of the state, and restore American preeminence?

Citizens today have potent weapons—the Internet, social networks, and viral media—to contest the dominance of elite opinion, and they are learning to use them. It will be a long time before the public abdicates their power and passively defers to elected representatives again.

So far, the movement for political reform has been fairly unstructured. There has been momentary advantage in appealing to public anger and distress over the current state of our politics and political institutions.

But we have seen how transitory this is. We have seen what happens when we merely substitute one set of opportunists or one ideological extreme for another. The people now demand results, and they don't care what party delivers them. The shelf life of an American politician or a majority party is no longer what it used to be.

The affections and support of the American public are up for grabs. Only a minority of Americans are *positively* affiliated with either political party. They are either driven by contempt for the extremes presented by the opposition, or they choose to be independents. However, any party or movement that can realign itself with the shared aspirations of the American people and advocate policies based on the broad public interest will find a receptive audience.

The American people have made it clear what they don't want. Now we have to do the heavy lifting and develop the plans, programs, structures, and strategies to redirect our vast human and material resources and resume the country's historic trajectory. To see the results of neglect, disunity, and lost vision, we need only look to the once-golden state of California. The laboratory of America is fast becoming an experiment gone wrong—a cautionary example for all.

We have allowed politics in America to devolve into a scrum where the extreme left and right fruitlessly seek to out-muscle each other in furious competition intent on "taking America back"—to places few of us want to go. Ultimately, energy is dissipated, resources are wasted, and we, the people, get nowhere.

To the American people, politics is not a game. The world is an increasingly dangerous place. We need its indispensable nation strong and our people united. We need America to come home.

We are a country of countries, each of us indivisible and sovereign. We will not be taken, only freely led. We seek a return to the path that once brought us together and carried us forward to a shared horizon, the one that *has* made all the difference.

The American tea party is far from over. Our country is a work in progress. Those who recently took to the streets, flocked to town halls, walked precincts, and manned phone banks are doing the work of democracy. They are part of a movement and a moment that started in Boston over two centuries ago. The movement endures. The moment persists. The party continues. Invitation is open.

All we have to do is change places.

Epilogue

All the art of living lies in a fine mingling of letting go
and holding on.

Havelock Ellis

I HAD THE GOOD fortune to be descended from people who followed their
dreams and sought opportunity in America. I was raised by devoted
parents and received a remarkable education. I lived through a period
of profound change, participated directly in the transformation of three
major institutions, and contested for one of America's highest political
offices.

I learned many lessons, but one stands out: Leadership matters. A
complex society such as ours by necessity must concentrate power in large
institutions, none larger or with greater capacities and attendant responsibilities than government. America was blessed by visionary leadership
in the original establishment of its government, and by an extraordinary
capability to inspire continuing devotion and fidelity to its founding principles and to raise up leaders of sufficient integrity, skill, and courage to
guide our country in times of great challenge.

Now our nation is again imperiled. Our position of global preeminence, our capacity to create opportunity, and our individual rights, the

most fundamental rationales for our system of government, are under unprecedented assault. The threat emanates not from some distant shore or from unbridgeable internal divisions. It comes, as it did some two hundred thirty-five years ago, from a governing aristocracy that has set itself apart, exceeded its legitimate authority, and promulgated laws and regulations that infringe upon our constitutional rights, limit opportunity, and undermine the birthright of our progeny.

Our political class has set us on an unsustainable course that, if not diverted, will bankrupt our country, destroy our way of life, and endanger the entire community of nations. Unless constrained, they will leave us with greater political, economic, and social division than at any time since the Civil War, and ultimately strip the world of the protection and inspiration of its one indispensable nation. We really are an exceptional country. From our first social contract, the Mayflower Compact, through our Declaration of Independence and the drafting of our Constitution, we have envisioned ourselves a people apart. Not only was our nation founded on unique principals, we are imbued with a singular sense of national moral purpose.

Through fidelity to those principles, America has achieved an absolute as well as relative degree of economic, military, political, and social influence unrivaled in human history. All humanity has benefited from our patrimony. We are not just a great people; we are a good people. We have made mistakes, to be sure, but they have generally been in the pursuit of honorable goals. We may not always merit the world's gratitude, but we certainly have nothing for which to apologize.

All of this has not come easily. Our history is one of struggle and sacrifice, first to earn and then to maintain our favored place in the constellation of nations. Today, we are called upon to meet different challenges. The US government is over two centuries old. Like all governments, it is a monopoly that suffers from lack of competition. It has grown inefficient, profligate, and subject to the corruptive influence of special interests. Worse, in recent years, as politics in America has become a business, our politicians have become technicians, professional only at the task of getting themselves elected and reelected. They substitute the rote ideology of party and political cant for sound reasoning and responsible leadership. The result is that too few people associated with government have the developed skills, experience, or motivation to set policy, or to actually lead and manage a complex organization and serve the shared interests of our diverse citizenry.

We live at a time of accelerated economic, social, and technological change. Is there any doubt that a federal government so poorly led, and one that now consumes fully a quarter of our national output, must also change? Compensating for years of failed leadership and mismanagement will require shared sacrifice by us all, to be sure, but little compared with the contributions of past generations. Fortunately, the solutions are well within our control. All we require is the will to join together once more in common cause to restore constitutional limits to our government, restructure the institutions of government consistent with changed circumstances, and elevate leaders of proven skill and integrity to make public service again live up to its name: performing service for the public.

Common-Sense Public Policy

Restructuring Government

Government does too many things, many of them poorly, and often for the wrong reasons. We must rein in a federal government that has grown too large and unfocused.

We need to restructure what our government does and how it does it:

1. We need a government that does only those things consistent with its enumerated powers that can't be done better by other means—a government that does only those things that the private sector can't do, won't do, or we wouldn't trust it to do.
2. We need a government that conducts its operations in accordance with normally accepted standards of efficiency, effectiveness, and honesty.

3. We need a government that represents all of our interests and bases its actions, consistent with our values as a society, on what produces the greatest good for the greatest number.

Much of what our government does evolved in response to past circumstances or the undue influence of special interests. Once government adopts a function, institutes a program, or creates an agency, that product takes on a life and constituency of its own, irrespective of its continued usefulness or legitimacy. We need a thorough reexamination and housecleaning of all the unnecessary functions and unproductive programs and structures adopted over the years that divert resources from the general welfare and sap the vitality of our economic system.

Establishing Standards

Once we decide what government should do and how it should be structured, there is no reason not to apply the same standards of performance that we would expect from any other institution. At minimum, we should reform the civil service so that the federal government can be run as a meritocracy.

Government should not cede any control over its operations or distort the procurement process for the contracting of goods and services in favor of any interest group. Like any other contractor, it should seek the lowest costs consistent with specified quality standards. For example, government employees may be entitled to seek or bargain for whatever compensation and work rules they wish, but union membership must be optional, dues collected privately, and arbitration noncompulsory. Uncompetitive practices and special interest–induced distortions, like paying the above-market "prevailing wage" for government construction, purchase of prescription drugs at above-market prices for Medicare, and special minority set-asides, should be abolished.

Further, it is essential that we reestablish high fiduciary standards in the conduct of our public affairs. It is incomprehensible that we tolerate conflicts of interest among our public officials that would merit dismissal or criminal indictment in the private sector. Clearly, we must be more exacting in our selection of both elected and appointed people, but there are institutional changes that we can implement, too.

To make the legislative process more honest, we should take the business of estimating program costs and projecting benefits out of the hands of self-interested politicians and instead establish a professional, nonpartisan, independent agency to analyze the financial impact of legislation and regulations proposed by elected officials and government bureaucrats. We should institute a presidential line-item veto to ensure at least one individual's accountability for spending, minimize legislative log-rolling, and assure that legislation is passed on its merits and not as the result of barter among the political caste. We should end all other special interest–directed legislation, like specific industry subsidies, arbitrary exemptions and bailouts, targeted tax breaks, and legislative earmarks. And the time has come to move beyond affirmative action and quotas and treat all Americans equally on their merits.

Since we must by necessity place great power in the hands of our elected and appointed officials, if we are to reestablish confidence in our leaders, we must be able to verify that they merit their positions and our trust. We must have real transparency in all government activities outside of national security. This will better enable the national press to report the actions of all public officials and hold them accountable to the highest ethical and professional standards, regardless of their ideologies.

Providing National Defense

The defense budget is too large. We need a total reappraisal of our defense strategy and annual expenditures that are currently multiples of the budgets of our potential military rivals. In national defense, we must determine the optimal potential projection of our military power internationally consistent with the paramount concerns of providing security at home, meeting our non-defense needs and maintaining our economic security. We are a beacon of freedom and self-determination, not crusading imperialists who seek to impose our ideology or ideals on others. The better we promote and honor our ideals, and the greater our achieved economic and social results at home, the more readily our example will appeal to others abroad.

We should:

1. Maintain sufficient capacity to address a serious distur-bance to international order, such as invasion of one coun-try into another in potential hot spots like the Middle East and North Korea. We should stay out of the internal affairs of other countries. We ourselves fought a revolution and a bloody civil war. While we should continue to resist geno-cide, there are certain things that nations must settle for themselves, unfortunately often through violent means.

2. Expand participation in organizations committed to the long-term maintenance of collective security and shared defense costs (e.g., NATO).

3. Stop the indiscriminate arming of those likely to become future enemies.

4. Seek to build coalitions willing to join together to punish nuclear proliferation. There is no useful purpose to expand-ing the nuclear "club." Nuclear weapons are a blight on the world. We must contain them. If someday we can find a way to eliminate them, we should.

5. Reexamine our financial and manpower commitments to Iraq and Afghanistan. We entered Iraq largely as a result of faulty intelligence. We clearly made a mistake; the Ba'ath regime was not an imminent threat. We are scheduled to remove all of our military personnel from the country within the next year, and we should do so. We entered Afghanistan to remove a regime that trained and harbored the terrorists most responsible for the 9/11 attacks on our country. That regime has been removed. If it returns or if its replacement resumes the support of terrorism, we can remove them again. The questions that we must answer are: How exactly is our national interest served by continued

involvement with this tribal culture? It is not sufficient to say that if we leave, those who died will have died in vain. If we stay longer, is it worth the further loss of life?

6. Seal our southern border with Mexico. What has become known as our "undocumented-immigrant problem" begs a larger question. How could we allow nearly 10 million people, however peacefully, to "invade" our country? Setting aside immigration policy, as an issue of national security, this is an abject and inexcusable failure. It is high time that those responsible perform the basic functions of protecting us from further invasion and stopping the unauthorized migration of individuals into our country.

Refocusing Foreign Policy

We must reappraise our foreign policy objectives and structures, consistent with changes in technology and the geopolitical environment.

We should:

1. Make a national commitment and create a coalition of nations to contain political Islam, similar to the commitment made to contain communism during the Cold War. Expansionist, militant, totalitarian Islam is no less a threat to world peace and security than expansionist, militant, totalitarian communism during the period following the Second World War. We did not choose to make an enemy of these people, but clearly they are dedicated to our destruction and that of Western civilization. We are fools not to recognize this, respond, and form coalitions to contain this deadly threat.

2. Restructure our relationship with the United Nations. The United Nations is a corrupt, hypocritical, and largely ineffective organization. Unless it is thoroughly restructured, we should limit the dimensions of future American participation to include only programs for education, public

health, and humanitarian assistance. We should withdraw from any form of involvement that purports to control, limit, or sanction the future conduct of the foreign policy of the United States of America. We should instead conduct all nonunilateral US foreign policy initiatives through bilateral, regional, and other ad hoc organizations and structures of our own design and choosing.

3. Reexamine the terms for United States participation in the World Trade Organization and negotiate bilateral trade relationships with large trading partners like China, where unsustainable trade and artificial currency imbalances persist. We are the world's largest market. This is a national resource that others benefit from accessing. We should treat it as such.

Evaluating and Designing Domestic Programs

We must establish the sustainable dimensions and terms of a new comprehensive American social safety net. We Americans have a history of taking care of our own, but our efforts have become unfocused and unresponsive to changed demographics and circumstances. Also, there is too little emphasis on helping people actualize their potential to become self-sufficient contributors to society.

We should:

1. Implement common-sense gradual change in our entitlement system that will assure long-term solvency consistent with changed demographics, without creating abrupt short-term change in individual circumstances.

2. Repeal the recently enacted and comprehensively flawed federal health-care law and define the terms and make provision for a minimum affordable and sustainable level of health care available for all citizens.

3. Analyze each of our various social welfare programs, eliminate the ineffective ones, consolidate the remainder, and

construct a coordinated and comprehensive system to help move individuals and families to self-sufficiency and fuller participation in society.

The motive force of our society has long been the hunger of the individual for personal liberty and the efforts of those at the middle and lower ends of the economic spectrum to create better lives for themselves and their families. We have been a beacon of freedom and a pathway to opportunity for untold millions, who have left home and country to lay the foundations and build out the City on a Hill first envisioned by our forefathers. As such we are a nation of, by, and for immigrants. The process of absorbing the world's huddled masses has not always been pretty or easy for us or them, but it is a singular source of our continuing strength and exceptionalism.

It is imperative that we take affirmative steps to resolve the legal status, terms of residency, and ultimate path (if any) to citizenship for all the undocumented residents among us. It is true that these people broke the law, but many have become an integral part of our economic and social fabric. We are simply not going to expel them indiscriminately. But neither can we continue to have millions of people roaming around our country in some legal no-man's-land. We should begin addressing this situation by granting all undocumented residents one final opportunity to comply with federal law. We could establish a new "provisional resident" immigration status and allow all undocumented residents one year to register. Any undocumented person found in the United States after that period would be subject to deportation without appeal. The initial terms of this provisional residency would be purposefully undefined. There would be no guarantees. They would provide no specific grace period for continued residency and establish no immediate "path to citizenship". They would merely confer "current" legal status to the recipient. Over the long term, through future acts, the United States Congress would at its discretion determine the rights, obligations, conditions, and term for continued residency as well as the ultimate disposition of these provisional residents.

Creating an Environment for Economic Growth and Opportunity

We should recognize that it is not the function of government to create jobs. It borders on laughable to hear public officials discourse on how they can and will create employment. Governments can only help provide an environment conducive for the private sector to produce economic growth, innovation, competitiveness, and, ultimately, productive jobs. There are several things that we should do to improve our prospects for economic growth:

1. Restructure publicly funded education through the application of technology and best practices, and inspire innovation and competition through the promotion of decentralized charter-type school organizations.
2. Maximize energy production and independence through full development of our hemispheric resources.
3. Implement tort reform and regulatory review.
4. Develop a national infrastructure plan.

Wrangling over the temporary tax cuts initiated by the Bush administration has given politicians of both parties an excuse to avoid the real fiscal issue: the composition and amount of federal spending. The Bush tax cuts became a welcome diversion for partisan political posturing. We should take *all* the Bush cuts (for the middle class as well as the "wealthy") off the table and let them expire as currently scheduled. Once we have restructured the government and determined our strategies for the future, we can analyze our revenue requirements, and then take up the issue of the best ways to raise them. As a general rule, the government should collect at minimum that level of taxes and fees consistent with maintaining its triple-A credit rating.

As presently constituted, the US tax code is a disgrace. Middle-class citizens and small businesses, in particular, should not require the expensive services of lawyers and accountants just to calculate their tax liability. Tax considerations should not be shaping our investment decisions. Neither should we have to employ a policing authority to enforce compliance. We have already established the principle that there should be progressivity in our tax code, not for reasons of fairness, but because as a practical matter, those with an ability to pay more are willing to do so. There is no determinable "fair" level of progressivity, only one that is politically palatable and economically sustainable. Once we determine how much revenue and how much progressivity is optimal, we should simplify, optimize, and make transparent our personal and corporate income tax system.

Our states and municipalities are presently burdened by above-market employee contracts and extraordinary benefit obligations promulgated by the past actions of self-serving politicians. For many government entities, there exist no reasonable prospects for honoring their commitments over the long term. However, to meet current obligations, they are deferring infrastructure investment and curtailing services vital to the public welfare. We must pass legislation that affords these governments the opportunity to seek court protection, restructure their financial obligations and operations, and resume that level of services necessary to support economic growth and access to opportunity.

Accepting Differences on Social Issues

We recognize that there exist widely divergent and legitimate differences among individual Americans with respect to many social issues. For too long, we have allowed views of these issues to dictate the terms of our electoral politics. This is problematic, since government has little standing as an arbiter in matters of faith and morals, and our politicians have virtually no influence on the public in these matters. Our differences can only be reconciled in the court of public opinion, not in the partisan political arena. We accept in good faith the differences among us in these personal matters and affirm the rights and interests of individuals in seeking wider public consensus supportive of their personal beliefs. However, we recognize the limits of government's role: to support the compromises that society, however haltingly, achieves.

America cannot be governed by extremes, nor reformed by bipartisan division of the spoils. Only leadership independent of the special interests and free of the ideological extremists that control our two major political parties can fashion the policies and programs necessary to restructure and redirect our government.

Only nonpartisan common-sense policies aimed at creating the greatest good for the greatest number and involving shared investment can elicit that level of public support required to institute sustainable positive change in our democracy.

And only an actively engaged, informed, vigilant, and independent citizenry can provide that animating force necessary to assure that government of, by, and for the people continues and flourishes, and that our great and good country fulfills its manifest promise.

Acknowledgments

MATERIAL DESCRIBING THE HISTORY and responsibilities of flight attendants is based on *Conquest of the Skies* by Carl Solberg, Little,
Brown and Company, 1979; "Lofty Ambitions" by Diana Atchison,
Commercial Appeal, July 1, 1990; and *Frequent Flyer* by Bob Reiss,
Simon & Schuster, 1994. *Frequent Flyer* supplied additional source
material for descriptions of the pilot, dispatcher, and meteorologist
professions.

Chapters One and Two are based on a first draft by Brian O'Connor.
Doris Kearns Goodwin and Linda Vandegrift conducted valuable research
of published materials, legal documents, and congressional testimony related to Northwest Airlines and the airline industry.

I am particularly indebted to Lisa Ross for editing the manuscript,
Stephanie Van de Wetering for technical support, and Rafael Beer for
book design and photographic composition.

Scott Wheeler offered valuable editorial comment. I am indebted
also to many friends who read drafts and offered helpful comments and
encouragement: Ed Abbott, Bob Burkett, Cheryl and Peter Barnes, Lucy
Gies, Jessica Makovsky, Al Michaels, Bill Scanlon, Jeffrey Rosenthal,
Scott Turow, and Jerry West.

My wife, Kathy, as always, served as an infinite source of patience,
support, and restraint.

Index

copyright © 2011 by Al Checchi

cover design by Jason Gabbert
interior design by Danielle Young

ISBN 978-1-4532-5822-4

Published in 2011 by Open Road Integrated Media
180 Varick Street
New York, NY 10014
www.openroadmedia.com